What important changes could be made in our culture to produce a higher percentage of emotionally healthy children and adults?

Adults should devote their creative energies to the teaching of *love* and *dignity*. Can boys and girls be taught to respect their peers? They certainly can! Young people are naturally more sensitive and empathetic than adults. Their viciousness is a learned response, resulting from the highly competitive and hostile world which their leaders have permitted to develop.

May I suggest to parents, *defend the underdog in your neighborhood.* Let it be known that you have the confidence to speak for the outcast. Explain this philosophy to your neighbors, and try to create an emotional harbor for the little children whose ship has been threatened by a storm of rejection. There is no more worthy investment of your time and energy.

DR. DOBSON ANSWERS YOUR QUESTIONS:
Confident Families

LIVING BOOKS®
Tyndale House Publishers, Inc.
Wheaton, Illinois

ACKNOWLEDGEMENTS

It is with gratitude that I hereby acknowledge the assistance of four women who contributed significantly to the production of this book. They are *Virginia Muir,* Senior Editor at Tyndale House Publishers, who assembled original material from my prior writings and recordings; *Dee Otte,* my Administrative Assistant, who kept the wheels turning when they would otherwise have ground to a halt; *Teresa Kvisler,* who typed and collated the final manuscript; and of course, my beloved wife, *Shirley,* who is an active partner in everything I do. Without the encouragement and dedication of these four members of the "team," a half finished manuscript would remain hopelessly buried beneath a mountain of paper on my desk.

Living Books is a registered trademark of Tyndale House Publishers, Inc.

Dr. Dobson Answers Your Questions about Confident, Healthy Families is selections from *Dr. Dobson Answers Your Questions,* copyright © 1982 by James C. Dobson, published by Tyndale House Publishers, Inc.

Excerpts from *Emotions: Can You Trust Them?* by Dr. James Dobson, copyright © 1980, published by Regal Books, a division of Gospel Light Publications, Ventura, CA 93006, used by permission.

Excerpts from *Hide or Seek* by Dr. James Dobson, copyright © 1974, 1979, published by Fleming H. Revell Company, Old Tappan, NJ 07675, used by permission.

Excerpts from *Straight Talk to Men and Their Wives* by Dr. James C. Dobson, copyright © 1980, published by Word Books, Waco, TX 76796, used by permission.

Scripture quotations marked TLB are taken from *The Living Bible,* copyright © 1971 owned by assignment by KNT Charitable Trust. All rights reserved.

Scripture quotations marked NIV are from the *Holy Bible,* New International Version. Copyright © 1973, 1978, 1984 International Bible Society. Used by permission of Zondervan Bible Publishers.

Scripture quotations marked RSV are from the *Holy Bible,* Revised Standard Version. Old Testament section, copyright 1952; New Testament section, first edition, copyright 1946; New Testament section, second edition, © 1971 by the Division of Christian Education of the National Council of the Churches of Christ in the United States of America.

Library of Congress Catalog Card Number 86-50759
ISBN 0-8423-1105-X

Printed in the United States of America

98 97 96 95 94 93 92
9   8   7   6   5   4   3   2   1

This book is affectionately dedicated to the professional colleagues and staff members who help me direct the activities of our nonprofit ministry, Focus on the Family. Paul Nelson, Gil Moegerle, Peb Jackson, Rolf Zettersten, Mike Trout, and 360 other coworkers and friends are deeply devoted to the principles and values expressed throughout this book.

It is entirely appropriate, therefore, that I take this opportunity to thank them for their diligent efforts to preserve the institution of the family.

CONTENTS

INTRODUCTION

During the summer of 1981, my family joined two others on a white water rafting trip down the beautiful Rogue River in Oregon. Those three days of churning water and blistering sun turned out to be one of the most exciting experiences of our lives . . . and perhaps my last! Just before departing on the journey I was told by our host, Dr. Richard Hosley, that "the river is always boss." Forty-eight hours later I learned what he meant.

Rather than floating on the raft for fifty miles in relative serenity and safety, I chose to paddle along behind in a plastic eight-foot canoe. And on the second afternoon, I insisted on rowing into the most treacherous part of the river. It was a bad decision.

Ahead lay a section of water known as the "Coffeepot," so named because the narrowing of the rock-walled banks created an unpredictable, bubbling current that had been known to suck small boats below the surface without warning. In fact, one unfortunate raftsman drowned in that area last summer. Nevertheless, I paddled toward the rapids with confidence (and blissful ignorance.)

I seemed to be handling the task quite well for the first few moments, before everything suddenly came unraveled. I was hit unexpectedly by the backwash flowing over a large rock and was unceremoniously thrown into the turbulent water. It seemed like an eternity before I came to the surface, only to find breathing impossible. A bandana that had been around my neck was now plastered across my mouth and was held there by my glasses. By the time I clawed free and gasped for air, another wave hit me in the face, sending half the river into my lungs. I came up coughing and sputtering before taking another unscheduled trip below the surface. By then I was desperate for air and keenly aware that the Coffeepot was only twenty-five yards downstream.

A kind of panic gripped me that I had not experienced since childhood! Although my life jacket probably guaranteed my survival, I definitely considered the possibility that I was drowning. My family and friends watched helplessly from the raft as

I bobbed through the rapids into the narrowest section of the river.

Through incredible rowing skill, Dr. Hosley managed to "hold" the raft until I could float alongside and grab the rope that rims the upper exterior structure. Then, as we were thrown from one side of the river to another, I pulled my feet up and sprang off the rocks and into the raft, avoiding a crushing blow against the vertical walls of the bank. I can assure you that I rode for several miles in the safety of the raft before moving a muscle!

The only lasting casualty of the experience is a matter of collegiate pride. Dr. Hosley was wearing a shirt with his beloved Stanford University named across the front. It survived the trip. But somewhere on the bottom of the Rogue River in shame and dishonor lies a watersoaked hat bearing the logo of the University of Southern California. It was a sad moment in the historic rivalry between the two alma maters!

After the crisis had passed, I reflected on the utter helplessness I had felt as the river's toy. My life was totally out of control and nothing could be taken for granted, not even a breath of air. Then my thoughts turned to the similar panic that is expressed so often in my counseling practice and in letters that are sent to my office. I currently receive thousands of letters per day, many of which reflect the same helplessness and lack of control I felt in the Rogue River. In fact, the analogy to "drowning" is certainly appropriate in this context; anxious people often use that precise term to describe the experience of being inundated in drug abuse, infidelity, alcoholism, divorce, physical disabilities, mental illness, adolescent rebellion, or low self-esteem. And immediately downstream are even greater dangers and threats.

Not all of the people who express this kind of anxiety are adults who have had time to mature and perceive life from a grown-up perspective. Some are children and adolescents who are trying to cope with problems in the best way possible. And for many today, their only alternative seems to be the ultimate self-hatred of suicide. Consider the following letter I received last year from a bewildered young man whom I'll call Roger.

Dear Dr. Dobson:
Hi, I'm 11 years old. I'm going in 6th grade. I just got done reading your

book, "Preparing for Adolescence." I want you to know it helped me.

When I was in 5th grade I was going with this girl. She broke up with me. *I had family problems.* [Italics mine.] So I tried to hang myself. Well I got a really bad pain in my neck. Then I got to where I couldn't breathe. I realized I wanted to live. So I yanked the noose off. And now God and I are struggling together.

Love, Roger

P.S. I didn't go into drugs and I never will. I have been asked but I say no. Some people respect me, others think I'm chicken. I don't care.

Each desperate letter of this nature I receive represents thousands of individuals with similar problems who do not bother to write. And at the core of their vast reservoir of misery lies the great common denominator of turmoil within the family. (Note Roger's vague reference to his problems at home. One can imagine its pivotal role in his attempted suicide.) The American family is experiencing an unprecedented period of disintegration which threatens the entire superstructure of our society, and we simply *must* take whatever steps are necessary to insure its integrity.

The urgency of this mission has become the predominant passion of my professional life. My greatest desire is to serve the God of my fathers by contributing to the stability and harmony of individual families in every way possible. If I can prevent just *one* child from experiencing the nightmare of parental conflict and divorce and custody hearings and wretching emotional pain, then my life will not have been lived in vain. If I can snatch a *single* fellow traveler from the turbulent waters that threaten to take him under, then there is purpose and meaning to my work. If I can lead but one lost human being to the personhood of Jesus Christ—the giver of life itself—then I need no other justification for my earthly existence.

That brings us to the book you are about to read, which is a product of the mission I've described. The philosophy underlying the recommendations offered is based on the best psychological information now available, in keeping with the commandments and values provided by the Creator Himself.

I hope you find this book helpful, whether you are currently gasping for air or floating high above the rapids. Thanks for your interest in our work, and may God continue to bless your home.

James Dobson, Ph.D.
Associate Clinical Professor of Pediatrics
USC School of Medicine

SECTION ONE

The Source of Self-Esteem in Children

Why are feelings of inadequacy and inferiority so prevalent among people of all ages at this time?

The current epidemic of self-doubt has resulted from a totally unjust and unnecessary system of evaluating human worth now prevalent in our society. Not everyone is seen as worthy; not everyone is accepted. Instead, we reserve our praise and admiration for a select few who have been blessed from birth with the characteristics we value most highly. It is a vicious system, and we, as parents, must counterbalance its impact.

It seems that human worth in our society is carefully reserved for those who meet certain rigid specifications. The beautiful people are born with it; those who are highly intelligent are likely to find approval; superstar athletes are usually respected. But no one is considered valuable just because he *is!* Social acceptability is awarded rather carefully, making certain to exclude those who are unqualified.[1]

When you speak of "rigid specifications" on which human worth is evaluated, what characteristics rank the highest to us?

At the top of the list of the most highly respected and valued attributes in our culture is *physical attractiveness*. Those who happen to have it are often honored and even feared; those who do not may be disrespected and rejected through no fault of their own. Though it seems incredibly unfair, this measure of human worth is evident from the earliest moments of life, when an attractive infant is considered more valuable than a homely one. For this reason, it is not uncommon for a mother to be very depressed shortly after the birth of her first baby. She knew that most newborns are rather ungainly, but she hadn't expected such a disaster! In fact, she had secretly hoped to give birth to a grinning, winking, blinking six-week old Gerber baby, having four front teeth and rosy, pink cheeks. Instead, they hand her a red, toothless, bald, prune-faced, screaming little creature whom she often wants to send back. You see, the personal worth of that one-day-old infant is actually doubted by his parents.

As the child grows, his value as a person will be assessed not only by his parents, but also by those outside his home. Beauty contests offering scholarships and prizes for gorgeous babies are now common, as if the attractive child didn't already have enough advantages awaiting him in life. This distorted system of evaluating human worth can be seen in a thousand examples. You may recall the tragic incident that occurred in Chicago during the sixties, when eight student nurses were viciously murdered. The following day, a commentator was discussing the violent event on the radio, and he said, "the thing that makes this tragedy much worse is that all eight of these girls were so attractive!" In other words, the girls were more valuable human beings because of their beauty, making their loss more tragic. If one accepts that statement, then the opposite is also true: the murders would have been less tragic if homely girls were involved. The conclusion, as written by George Orwell, is inescapable: "All [people] are equal, but some [people] are more equal than others."

My point is that from the earliest experience of life, a child begins to learn the social importance of physical beauty. The values of his society cannot be kept from his little ears, and many adults do not even try to conceal their bias.[2]

How do feelings of inferiority get started? It seems as though I've always felt inadequate, but I can't remember where it all began.

You don't remember it because your self-doubt originated during your earliest days of conscious existence. A little child is born with an irrepressible inclination to question his own worth; it is as "natural" as his urge to walk and talk. At first, it is a primitive assessment of his place in the home, and then it extends outward to his early social contacts beyond the front door. These initial impressions of who he is have a profound effect on his developing personality, particularly if the experiences are painful. It is not uncommon for a prekindergartner to have concluded already that he is terribly ugly, incredibly dumb, unloved, unneeded, foolish, or strange.

These early feelings of inadequacy may remain relatively tranquil and subdued during the elementary school years. They lurk just below the conscious mind and are never far from awareness. But the child with the greatest self-doubts constantly "accumulates" evidence of his inferiority during these middle years. Each failure is recorded in vivid detail. Every unkind remark is inscribed in his memory. Rejection and ridicule scratch and nick his delicate ego all through the "quiet" years. Then it happens! He enters adolescence and his world explodes from within. All of the accumulated evidence is resurrected and propelled into his conscious mind with volcanic forcefulness. He will deal with that experience for the rest of his life. Have you done the same?[3]

Why do people seem to be more conscious of their physical flaws and inadequacies now than in the past? What accounts for the "epidemic" of inferiority which you described?

I believe this tremendous emphasis on physical attractiveness is a by-product of the sexual revolution going on around us.

Our society has been erotically super-charged since the mid-sixties when the traditional moral standards and restraints began to collapse. Television, radio, magazines, movies, billboards, literature and clothing all reflect this unparalleled fascination with sensuality of various sorts. Now obviously, when sex becomes all-important in a society, as we are witnessing, then each person's sex appeal and charm take on new social significance. Simply stated, the more steamed up a culture becomes over sex, the more it will reward beauty and punish ugliness.

It is my view that the increased sensuality in America during the seventies and eighties is generating a higher incidence of emotional casualties among people who are intensely aware of their inability to compete in the flirtatious game. If beauty represents the necessary currency (the gold coin of worth), then they are undeniably bankrupt. And sadly, the most vulnerable victims of this foolish measure of human worth are the little children who are too young to understand, too immature to compensate, and too crushed to fight back.[4]

I understand how society evaluates the worth of a child on the basis of his

physical attractiveness. But how does *he* learn of that assessment so early? By what mechanism does this cultural attitude get transmitted to preschool kids?

They can hardly miss it in the world around them. It's a dull child who fails to notice that the ugly do not win Miss America contests; the ugly do not become cheerleaders; the ugly seldom star in movies; the ugly may not get married; the ugly have fewer friends; the ugly are less desirable! Furthermore, in examining the traditional literature of childhood, I am amazed to see how many of the age-old stories center around physical attractiveness in one form or another. Consider these examples:

The Ugly Duckling. Here is a familiar story about an unhappy little bird who was rejected by the better-looking ducks. The ugly duckling was disturbed by his grotesque appearance. Fortunately for him, however, he had a beautiful swan inside which surfaced in young adulthood. (The story does not mention the ugly duckling who grew up to be an ugly duck!) How many children wait patiently for their beautiful swan to appear, seeing things go from bad to worse during adolescence?

Rudolph the Red-Nosed Reindeer. Rudolph had a weird nose which caused him to be rejected by his fellow reindeer. This story has nothing to do with reindeer; it has everything to do with children. This is how they treat the physically peculiar. They are rejected and ridiculed. The only way the world's "Rudolphs" can gain acceptance is to perform some miraculous feat, symbolized by the gallant sleigh ride in the snowstorm.

Dumbo the Elephant. Dumbo was ridiculed for having big floppy ears, until he used them to fly. The theme is remarkably similar to the plight of poor Rudolph. It appears repeatedly in the literature of the young because of its common occurrence in the lives of children themselves.

Snow White and the Seven Dwarfs. The evil queen asked the fateful question, "Mirror, mirror on the wall, who's the fairest of them all?" I am still awed by the crassness of her question considering all of the possibilities to which a magic mirror might respond! Yet the motivation behind her request is clear: the fairest of them all was the most noble, worthy person in the land. Perhaps she still reigns.

Cinderella. The primary difference between Cinderella and her two wicked stepsisters was a matter of beauty. Any illustrated story of Cinderella will reveal that fact. Sure, Cinderella was ragged and uncombed, but the basic ingredient was there. It wasn't the pumpkin and the mice that shook up the prince when Cinderella arrived at the ball. You can bet she was a pretty little thing.

My point is that we are incredibly effective in teaching very young children the importance of personal beauty. *All* children learn it shortly after babyhood! We could do no better if our best educators convened to design a fool proof instructional system.[5]

What role do teachers play in emphasizing the importance of physical attractiveness?

Unfortunately, teachers are products of the same society which molds the values and attitudes of everyone else. They are often repelled by the physically unattractive child and drawn to the cutie.

Two researchers, Ellen Berscheid and Elaine Walster, published their startling findings in a classic article, "Beauty and the Best," in *Psychology Today* (March 1972). Consider the impact of these biases against the homely youngster.

> 1. Evidence seems to include that academic grades given to students are

influenced by the attractiveness of the child.

2. When shown a set of children's pictures and asked to identify the child who probably created the classroom disturbance (or some similar act of misconduct), adults were likely to select an unattractive child as the offender. Likewise, the ugly child was thought to be more dishonest than his cute peer.

3. According to the findings of Karen Dion, the way an adult handles a discipline problem is related to the attractiveness of the child. In other words, the *same* misbehavior is likely to be handled more permissively for the cute youngster and more severely for his ugly classmate.

4. Most important (and correlating with my observations), the impact of physical attractiveness is well established in nursery school! Cute little three-year-olds already enjoy greater popularity among their peers. And unfortunately, certain physical features, such as fatness, are already recognized and disliked at this tender age.[6]

What are the prospects for the very pretty or handsome child? Does he usually have smooth sailing all the way?

He has some remarkable advantages, as I have described. He is much more likely to accept himself and enjoy the benefits of self-confidence. However, he also faces some unique problems which the homely child never experiences. Beauty in our society is power, and power can be dangerous in immature hands. A fourteen-year-old nymphet, for example, who is prematurely curved and rounded in all the right places may be pursued vigorously by males who would exploit her beauty. As she becomes more conscious of her flirtatious power, she is sometimes urged toward promiscuity. Furthermore, women who have been coveted physically since early childhood, such as Marilyn Monroe or Brigitte Bardot, may become bitter and disillusioned by the depersonalization of body worship.

Research also indicates some interesting consequences in regard to marital stability for the "beautiful people." In one important study, the more attractive college girls were found to be less happily married twenty-five years later. It is apparently difficult to reserve the "power" of sex for one mate, ignoring the ego gratification which awaits outside the marriage bonds. And finally, the more attractive a person is in his youth, the more painful is the aging process.

My point is this: the measurement of worth on a scale of beauty is wrong, often damaging both the "haves" and the "have-nots."[7]

What do teenagers most often dislike about themselves?

In a class study by E. A. Douvan, titled *Adolescent Girls,* nearly 2,000 girls from eleven to eighteen years of age were asked, "What would you most like to change about yourself if you could . . . your looks, your personality, or your life?" Fifty-nine percent mentioned some aspect of their physical appearance. (Only 4 percent desired greater ability.) The most common personal dissatisfaction for both boys and girls concerns facial defects, primarily skin problems. In a later study by H. V. Cobb, children in grades four to fourteen were asked to complete the sentence, "I wish I were": The majority of the boys answered "taller" and the girls answered "smaller." Certainly, there is a great volume of scientific evidence to document children's preoccupation and dissatisfaction with their own physical characteristics.[8]

You referred to a "system" of evaluating human worth in our culture, beginning with the most important attribute of physical attractiveness. What ranks second in significance?

It is the presence of intelligence, as expressed in scholastic aptitude. When the birth of a firstborn child is imminent, his parents pray that he will be normal . . . that is, "average." But from that moment on, average will not be good enough. Their child must excel. He must succeed. He must triumph. He must be the first of his age to walk or talk or ride a tricycle. He must earn a stunning report card and amaze his teachers with his wit and wisdom. He must star in Little League, and later he must be the quarterback or the senior class president or the valedictorian. His sister must be the cheerleader or the soloist or the homecoming queen. Throughout the formative years of childhood, his parents give him the same message day after day: "We're counting on you to do something fantastic, son, now don't disappoint us!"

According to Martha Weinman Lear, author of *The Child Worshippers,* the younger generation is our most reliable status symbol. Middle-class parents vigorously compete with each other in raising the best-dressed, best-fed, best-educated, best-mannered, best-medicated, best-cultured, and best-adjusted child on the block. The hopes, dreams, and ambitions of an entire family sometimes rest on the shoulders of an immature child. And in this atmosphere of fierce competition, the parent who produces an intellectually gifted child is clearly holding the winning sweepstakes ticket. As Lear says, "By the present line of thinking all children deserve the very best except the [intellectually] gifted, who deserve even better."

Unfortunately, exceptional children are just that—exceptions. Seldom does a five-year-old memorize the King James Version of the Bible, or play chess blindfolded, or compose symphonies in the Mozart manner. To the contrary, the vast majority of our children are not dazzlingly brilliant, extremely witty, highly coordinated, tremendously talented, or universally popular! They are just plain kids with oversized needs to be loved and accepted as they are. Thus, the stage is set for unrealistic pressure on the younger generation and considerable disappointment for their parents.[9]

You have stated that a majority of children emerge from the school systems with the conviction that they are unintelligent and stupid. Would you explain why this attack on self-worth affects so many kids today?

There are five large groups of children who consistently fail in the classroom, leading them (and their parents) to conclude that they are incapable. These broad categories are as follows:

1. *The slow learner.* This is the child who lacks an aptitude for academic work. He tries to do the assignments but nothing turns out right. He has difficulty learning to read in the first grade. He doesn't understand science. He rarely receives a "happy face" for doing things properly, and *never* has his teacher written "Nice work!" on his paper. He is the only child in the room who won't get a gold star on his spelling chart. And he is probably going to be retained in the same grade at least once, which convinces him of his stupidity!

2. *The semiliterate child.* This is the child in whose home two languages are spoken, but he has learned neither of them

very well. Thus, he is not "bilingual"—he is semiliterate. He may be so incapable of expressing himself that he rarely makes a sound unless compelled to talk. His progress in an English school will be an uphill struggle throughout his childhood.

3. *The underachiever.* This is the child who is bright but unself-disciplined and unmotivated to work. His school assignments are usually late, missing, sloppy, or foolish, leading him to draw the same weary conclusion: "I'm dumb!"

4. *The culturally deprived child.* This is a youngster from an impoverished neighborhood. He has never visited a zoo, ridden on a plane, or been fishing. His daddy's identity is a mystery and his mother works long hours to support five little children. His vocabulary is minuscule, except for an astounding array of slang words, and he has no place to read or study at home. He *knows* he isn't going to make it in school, and this fact is already influencing his personal evaluation.

5. *The late bloomer.* This is the immature child (usually a boy) who starts school before he is ready and experiences early failure. Though he may catch up in maturity, his lack of school success may handicap him throughout his school career.

It is appalling to recognize that the children in these five categories actually outnumber those students who feel successful in school! [10]

It is obvious that you think the attitudes and reactions of parents play a key role in the self-esteem of children.

Children are extremely vulnerable to the subtle attitude of their parents. That's why adults must learn to guard what they say in the presence of their children. How many times, following a speaking engagement, have I been consulted by a mother regarding a particular problem her child is having. As Mom describes the gritty details, I notice that the subject of all this conversation is standing about a yard behind her. His ears are ten feet tall as he listens to a candid description of all his faults. The child may remember that conversation for a lifetime.

It is clear that parents often convey disrespect to a child whom they genuinely love. For example, Mom may become tense and nervous when little Jimmy speaks to guests or outsiders. She butts in to explain what he is trying to say or laughs nervously when his remarks sound foolish. When someone asks him a direct question, she interrupts and answers for him. She reveals her frustration when she is trying to comb his hair or make him "look nice" for an important event. He knows she thinks it is an impossible assignment. If he is to spend a weekend away from the family, she gives him an extended lecture on how to avoid making a fool of himself. These subtle behaviors are signals to the child that his mother doesn't trust him with her image—that he must be supervised closely to avoid embarrassing the whole family. He reads disrespect in her manner, though it is framed in genuine love.

My point is that parents should be sensitive to the self-concept of their children, being especially mindful of matters pertaining to physical attractiveness or intelligence of the kids. These are two primary "soft spots" where boys and girls are most vulnerable.[11]

What are some of the factors that hinder parents from building their child's self-esteem?

In a very real sense, we parents are products of the society whose values I have condemned. We have systematically been taught to worship beauty and brains, as everyone else, and so have our grandmommas and grandpoppas and uncles and aunts and cousins and neighbors. We all want super-children who will amaze the world. Let's face it, folks: We have met the enemy, and it is *us*. Often the greatest damage is unintentionally inflicted right in the home, which should be the child's sanctuary and fortress. Furthermore, I have observed in working with parents that their *own* feelings of inferiority make it difficult for them to accept gross imperfections in their children. They don't intend to reject their sons and daughters, and they work hard to conceal these inner thoughts. But their "damaged" child symbolizes their own personal inadequacies and failures. Thus, it takes a very mature parent to look down upon an ugly child, or one who is clearly deficient in mentality, and say, "Not only do I love you, little one, but I recognize your immeasurable worth as a human being."

The first step in overcoming this bias is to examine your own feelings—even being willing to expose those guilt-laden attitudes which may have been unconscious heretofore. Are you secretly disappointed because your child is so ordinary? Have you rejected him, at times, because of his lack of appeal and charm? Do you think he is dumb and stupid? Was he born during a

difficult time, imposing financial and physical stress on the family? Did you want a
girl instead of a boy? Or a boy instead of a
girl? Was this child conceived out of wed-
lock, forcing an unwanted marriage? Do
you resent the freedom you lost when he
came or the demands he places on your
time and effort? Does he embarrass you by
being either too loud and rambunctious or
too inward and withdrawn?

Quite obviously, you can't teach a child to
respect himself when you dislike him for
reasons of your own! By examining your
inner-most feelings, perhaps with the help
of an understanding counselor or doctor,
you *can* make room in your heart as a
loving parent for your less-than-perfect
youngster. After all, what right do we have
to demand superchildren when we are so
ordinary ourselves![12]

**You have talked about the attributes
or characteristics which are most
highly valued in the Western culture.
But what is the source of self-esteem
itself?**

Feelings of self-worth and acceptance,
which provide the cornerstone of a healthy
personality, can be obtained from only *one*
source. It cannot be bought or manufac-

tured. Self-esteem is only generated by what we see reflected about ourselves in the eyes of other people or in the eyes of God. In other words, evidence of our worthiness must be generated *outside* of ourselves. It is only when others respect us that we respect ourselves. It is only when others love us that we love ourselves. It is only when others find us pleasant and desirable and worthy that we come to terms with our own egos. Occasionally, a person is created with such towering self-confidence that he doesn't seem to need the acceptance of other people, but he is indeed a rare bird. The vast majority of us are dependent on our associates for emotional sustenance each day. What does this say, then, about those who exist in a state of perpetual isolation, being deprived of loving, caring human contact year after year? Such people are virtually certain to experience feelings of worthlessness, accompanied by deep depression and despair.[13]

You say beauty and intelligence are the most critical factors in shaping self-esteem and confidence. What other influences contribute to the child's level of self-confidence?

Let me list some of the more common

variables that relate to self-worth in our culture:

1. Parents have a remarkable power to preserve or damage the self-esteem of a child. Their manner either conveys respect and love or disappointment and disinterest.

2. Older siblings can crush the confidence of a younger, weaker child. The little one can never run as fast, or fight as well, or achieve as much as his big brothers and sisters. And if his words are perpetually matters of scorn, he can easily conclude that he is foolish and incapable.

3. Early social blunders and mistakes are sometimes extremely painful, being remembered throughout a lifetime.

4. Financial hardship, depriving a child of the clothes and lifestyle of his peers, can cause a child to feel inferior. It is not the poverty, itself, which does the damage. Rather, it is the relative comparison with others. It is possible to feel deprived when you are truly rich by the world's standards. Incidentally, money is probably the third most important source of self-esteem in our culture. In the materialistic eyes of society, for example, a pimply-faced teenager on a bicycle is somehow considered less worthy

than a pimply-faced teenager in a Datsun 280Z.

5. Disease, even when unapparent, may represent the child's "inner flaw." A cardiac condition, or other disorder, which forces Mom to nag and beg him to slow down can convince a child that he is brittle and defective.

6. A child who has been raised in a protected environment, such as a farm or a foreign missionary outpost, may be embarrassed by his underdeveloped social skills. His tendency is to pull inward in shy withdrawal.

7. Embarrassing family characteristics, such as having an alcoholic father or a mentally retarded sibling, can produce feelings of inferiority through close identification with the disrespected relatives.

Unfortunately, this list could be almost endless. In working with the problem of inadequacy, I have drawn this conclusion: whereas a child can lose self-esteem in a thousand ways, the careful reconstruction of his personal worth is usually a slow, difficult process.

You have convinced me that beauty, brains, and materialism are false values that demoralize the self-esteem of

kids. But what will take their place? What values do you suggest that I teach to my children?

I believe *the* most valuable contribution a parent can make to his child is to instill in him a genuine faith in God. What greater ego satisfaction could there be than knowing that the Creator of the universe is acquainted with me, personally? That He values me more than the possessions of the entire world; that He understands my fears and my anxieties; that He reaches out to me in immeasurable love when no one else cares; that His only Son, Jesus, actually gave His life for me; that He can turn my liabilities into assets and my emptiness into fullness; that a better life follows this one, where the present handicaps and inadequacies will all be eliminated—where earthly pain and suffering will be no more than a dim memory! What a beautiful philosophy with which to "clothe" your tender child. What a fantastic message of hope and encouragement for the broken teenager who has been crushed by life's circumstances. This is self-esteem at its richest, not dependent on the whims of birth or social judgment, or the cult of the superchild, but on divine decree.[14]

SECTION TWO
Developing Self-Esteem in Children

I have a nine-year-old daughter who lacks confidence and self-respect. What can I do to help her?

One of the most productive means of instilling self-confidence is to teach methods by which the child can compensate. *Compensation* occurs when the individual counterbalances his weaknesses by capitalizing on his strengths. It is our job as parents to help our children find those strengths and learn to exploit them for all the self-satisfaction they will yield. And this brings us to a very important concept to be grasped: Inferiority can either crush and paralyze an individual, or it can provide tremendous emotional energy which powers every kind of success and achievement. Remember that the same boiling water that hardens the egg will soften the carrot. Everything depends on the individual's *reaction* to stressful circumstances.

The question is, will your daughter collapse under the weight of inferiority, or will she use her emotional needs to supercharge her initiative and drive? The answer may depend on the direction you can provide in identifying compensatory skills. Perhaps she can establish her niche in music—many children do. Maybe she can develop her artistic talent, or learn to write or cultivate mechanical skills, or learn to cook or raise rabbits for fun and profit. Regardless of what the choice is, the key is to start her down that road early— right now! There is nothing more risky than sending a teenager into the storms of adolescence with no skills, no unique knowledge, no means of compensating. When this occurs, her ego is stark naked. She cannot say, "I may not be the most popular student in school, but I am the best trumpet player in the band!" Her only source of self-esteem comes from the acceptance of other students—and their love is notoriously fickle.[1]

Can you explain the process of compensation in greater detail? How does it relate to feelings of low self-esteem?

The unconscious reasoning of a compensator goes like this:

> I refuse to be drowned in a sea of inferiority. I can achieve adequacy through my success if I work hard at it. Therefore, I will pour all my energy into basketball (or painting, or sewing, or politics, or graduate school, or gardening, or motherhood, or salesmanship, or Wall Street—or for a child, elementary school, or piano playing, or baton-twirling or football).

This kind of compensation provides the emotional energy for virtually every kind of successful human behavior, as described earlier. In a famous study by Victor and Mildred Goertzel, entitled *Cradles of Eminence,* the home backgrounds of four hundred highly successful people were investigated. These four hundred subjects were individuals who had made it to the top. They were men and women whose names you would recognize as brilliant or outstanding in their respective fields (Churchill, Gandhi, F. D. Roosevelt,

Schweitzer, Einstein, Freud, etc.). The intensive investigation into their early home lives yielded some surprising findings:

1. Three-fourths of the children [were] troubled—by poverty; by a broken home; by rejecting, over-possessive, estranged, or dominating parents; by financial ups and downs; by physical handicaps; or by parental dissatisfaction over the children's school failures or vocational choices.

2. Seventy-four of eighty-five writers of fiction or drama and sixteen of twenty poets [came] from homes where, as children, they saw tense psychological dramas played out by their parents.

3. Handicaps such as blindness; deafness; being crippled, sickly, homely, undersized, or overweight; or having a speech defect [occurred] in the childhoods of over one-fourth of the sample.

It seems very apparent that the need to compensate for their disadvantages was a major factor in their struggle for personal achievement. It may even have been *the* determining factor.

There have been thousands, perhaps millions, of inadequate persons who used compensation to achieve esteem and confidence. Perhaps the most classic illustration is seen in the life of Eleanor Roosevelt, the former First Lady. Being orphaned at ten, she underwent a childhood of utter anguish. She was very homely and never felt she really belonged to anybody. According to Victor Wilson, Newhouse News Service, "She was a rather humorless introvert, a young woman unbelievably shy, unable to overcome her personal insecurity and with a conviction of her own inadequacy." The world knows, however, that Mrs. Roosevelt did rise above her emotional shackles. As Wilson said, ". . . from some inner wellspring, Mrs. Roosevelt summoned a tough, unyielding courage, tempered by remarkable self-control and self-discipline. . . ." That "inner wellspring" has another appropriate name: compensation!

Obviously, one's *attitude* toward a handicap determines its impact on his life. It has become popular to blame adverse circumstances for irresponsible behavior; i.e., poverty *causes* crime, broken homes *pro-*

duce juvenile delinquents, a sick society imposes drug addiction on its youth. This fallacious reasoning removes all responsibility from the shoulders of the individual. The excuse is hollow. We must each decide what we will do with inner inferiority or outer hardship.

Admittedly, it requires courage to triumph despite unfavorable odds. Compensation takes guts, for some much more than others. The easier path is to wallow in self-pity—to freak-out on drugs—to hate the world—to run—to withdraw—to compromise. Regardless of the ultimate course of action, however, the choice is ours alone and no one can remove it from us. Hardship does not *determine* our behavior, but it clearly influences it.

Parents can and should open the door to responsible "choices" by giving their children the means by which to compensate, beginning during their middle childhood years.[2]

What is the *best* source of compensation for boys in this culture, especially for the kid who is "hurting" inside?

Because of the status athletes have in today's high schools, I believe this avenue of compensation should be explored by the parents of "high risk" boys. If a child is reasonably coordinated, he can be taught to play basketball, football, tennis, track, or golf. I have seen some of the most homely adolescents who were highly respected for helping Thomas Jefferson High School win the championship. As stated before, the key to athletic excellence is to give Junior an early start. We do not hesitate to provide piano lessons for our eight-year-olds; why should we not give basketball training at the same age?

My son is not athletically inclined. How can I as a parent decide what skill my son should develop? Shouldn't that choice be left to him?

Many parents feel they do not have the right to force a choice of this nature on their child. They sit back in the hopes that he will make it for himself. However, most children are remarkably unself-disciplined. It is always difficult to learn a new skill—particularly during the initial stages. There is no fun to be derived from total failure, which is the typical feeling in the beginning. Thus, the child never learns those important skills which he will need so badly later on. I recommend that you, his parent, make a careful assessment of his areas of strength.

Then select a skill where you believe the greatest possibilities for success lie. Once this selection is made, see to it that he gets through the first stage. Reward him, push him, threaten him, beg him—bribe him if necessary—but make him learn it. If you discover later that you've made a mistake, back up and start over on something else. But don't let inertia keep you from teaching something emotionally useful to your offspring! Does this form of coercion impinge upon the freedom of the child to choose for himself? Perhaps, but so does making him eat properly, keep himself clean, and go to bed at a reasonable hour. It is, as they say, in the child's best interest.[4]

What happens when a child is so different from the group that he cannot compete, no matter how hard he tries?

That dead-end street is most often responsible for attempts at self-destruction. I am reminded of a sad little girl named Lily, an eighth-grader who was referred to me for psychological counselling. She opened the door to my office and stood with eyes cast down. Underneath several layers of powder and make-up, her face was completely aglow with infected acne. Lily had done her best to bury the inflammation, but she had not been successful. She weighed about eighty-five pounds and was a physical wreck from head to toe. She sat down without raising her eyes to mine, lacking the confidence to face me. I didn't need to ask what was troubling her. Life had dealt her a devastating blow, and she was bitter, angry, broken, and deeply hurt. The teenager who reaches this point of despair can see no tomorrow. He has no hope. He can't think of anything else. He knows he is repulsive and disgusting. He would like to crawl in a hole, but there is no place to hide. Running away won't help, nor will crying change anything. Too often he chooses suicide as the only way out.

Lily gave me little time to work. The following morning she staggered into the school office and announced that she had internalized everything in the family medicine cabinet. We labored feverishly to retrieve the medication and finally succeeded on the way to the hospital. Lily survived physically, but her self-esteem and confidence had died years earlier. The scars on her sad face symbolized the wounds on her adolescent heart.

Obviously, the inability to gain social acceptance is not merely an uncomfortable feeling among the young; such lack of self-esteem can actually extinguish the desire to go on living. Parents and teachers must be taught to recognize the early symptoms of personal despair during the tender, pliable years of childhood, and more importantly, what they can do about it.[5]

I know children can be hateful and mean, especially to the handicapped child or one who is "different." This seems terribly destructive to kids who are especially vulnerable to ridicule. Do you agree that adults are responsible to intercede when a child is being attacked by his peers?

I certainly do and I am well aware of the danger you described. In fact, I lived it. When I was approximately eight years old, I attended a Sunday school class as a regular member. One morning a visitor entered our class and sat down. His name was Fred, and I can still see his face. More important, I can still see Fred's ears. They were curved in the shape of a reversed C, and protruded noticeably. I was fascinated by the shape of Fred's unusual ears because they reminded me of jeep fenders (we were deep into World War II at the time). Without thinking of Fred's feelings, I pointed out his strange feature to my friends, who all thought Jeep Fenders was a terribly funny name for a boy with bent ears. Fred seemed to think it was funny, too, and he chuckled along with the rest of us. Suddenly, Fred stopped laughing. He jumped to his feet, red in the face (and ears), and rushed to the door crying. He bolted into the hall and ran from the building. Fred never returned to our class.

I remember my shock over Fred's violent and unexpected reaction. You see, I had *no* idea that I was embarrassing him by my little joke. I was a sensitive kid and often defended the underdog, even when I was a youngster. I would *never* have hurt a visitor on purpose—and that is precisely my point. Looking back on the episode, I hold my teachers and my parents responsible for that event. They should have told me what it feels like to be laughed at . . . especially for something different about your body. My mother, who was very wise with children, has since admitted that she should have taught me to feel for others. And as for the Sunday school teachers, I don't remember what their curriculum consisted of at that time, but what better content could they have presented than the *real* meaning of the commandment, "Love they neighbor as thyself"?[6]

You implied that the "middle child" has greater problems with low self-esteem than other members of the family. Maybe that explains why my second son has never been a confident person.

Low self-esteem can become a problem for any human being, regardless of birth order or age. However, the middle child does sometimes find it more difficult to establish his identity within the family. He enjoys neither the status of the eldest nor the attention given to the baby. Furthermore, he is likely to be born at a busy period in the life of the parents, and especially his mother. Then when he reaches the toddler years, his precious territory is invaded by a cute little newborn who steals Mama from him. Is it any wonder that he often asks, "Who am I and where is my place in life?"

What can I do to help my middle child, who suffers from low self-esteem?

I would recommend that parents take steps to insure the identity of *all* their children, but especially the child in the middle. That can be accomplished by occasionally relating to each boy or girl as individuals, rather than merely as members of the group. Let me offer two suggestions that may serve as examples that well illustrate what I mean.

1. It is meaningful for Dad to "date" each child, *one at a time,* every four or five weeks. The other kids should not be told where they are going until it is revealed by the boy or girl in retrospect. They can play miniature golf, go bowling, play basketball, eat tacos or pizza, or visit a skating rink. The choice should be made by the child whose turn has arrived.

2. Ask each offspring to design his own flag, which can be sewn in canvas or cloth. That flag is then flown in the front yard on the child's "special" days, including birthdays, after he has received an A in school, when he scores a goal in soccer, or hits a home run in baseball, and so forth.

There are other ways to accomplish the same purpose. The target, again, is to plan activities that emphasize one child's individuality apart from his identity within the group.[8]

My son is an outstanding gymnast. His high school coach says he has more natural ability than anyone he's ever seen. Yet, when he is being judged in a competitive meet, he does terribly!

Why does he fail during the most important moments?

If your son thinks of himself as a failure, his performance will probably match his low self-image when the chips are down. In the same way, there are many excellent golfers in the PGA tour who make a satisfactory living in tournament play, but they never win. They consistently place second, third, sixth, or tenth. Whenever it looks like they might come in first, they "choke" at the last minute and let someone else win. It is not that they want to fail; rather, they don't "see" themselves as winners, and their performance merely reflects this image.

I talked recently with a concert pianist of outstanding talent who has resolved never to play in public again. She knows she is blessed with remarkable talent, but believes she is a loser in every other regard. Consequently, when she plays the piano on stage, her mistakes and errors make her sound like a beginner. Each time this mortifying experience has occurred, she has become more convinced of her own unworthiness in *every* area. She has now withdrawn into the secluded, quiet, talentless world of have-nots.

There is no question about it: a lack of

self-confidence can completely immobilize a talented person, simply through the threat of failure.[9]

Is this true of mental ability, too? My twelve-year-old was asked to recite a poem at a school function the other day, and he went completely blank in front of the crowd. I know he knew the poem perfectly because he said it dozens of times at home. He's a bright child, but he's had this trouble before. Why does his mind "turn off" when he's under pressure?

It will be helpful to understand an important characteristic of intellectual functioning. Your son's self-confidence, or the lack of it, actually affects the way his brain operates. All of us have experienced the frustration of mental "blocking," which you described. This occurs when a name or fact or idea just won't surface to the conscious mind, even though we *know* it is recorded in the memory. Or suppose we are about to speak to an antagonistic group and our mind suddenly goes blank. This kind of blocking usually occurs (1) when social pressure is great, and (2) when self-confidence is low. Why? *Because emotions affect the efficiency of the human brain.* Unlike a computer, our mental apparatus only functions properly when a delicate biochemical balance exists between the neural cells. This substance makes it possible for a cell to "fire" its electrochemical charge across the gap (synapse) to another cell. It is now known that a sudden emotional reaction can instantly change the nature of that biochemistry, blocking the impulse. This blockage prevents the electrical charge from being relayed and the thought is never generated. This mechanism has profound implications for human behavior; for example, a child who feels inferior and intellectually inadequate often does not even make use of the mental power with which he has been endowed. His lack of confidence produces a disrupting mental interference, and the two go around in an endless cycle of defeat. This is obviously what happened to your son when he "forgot" the poem.[10]

What can I do to help him?

Actually, it is not unusual for a twelve-year-old to "choke" in front of a crowd. I once stood before three hundred fellow teenagers with my words stuck in my throat and my mind totally out to lunch. It was a painful experience, but time gradually erased its impact. As your child matures, he will probably overcome the problem, if he can experience a few successes to build his confidence. Anything that raises self-esteem will reduce the frequency of mental blocking for children and adults alike.[11]

What kind of homes produce children with a high degree of self-confidence? Are there characteristics of the most wholesome families that we can try to emulate?

Dr. Stanley Coopersmith, associate professor of psychology, University of California, studied 1,738 normal middle-class boys and their families, beginning in the pre-adolescent period and following them through to young manhood. After identifying those boys having the highest self-esteem, he compared their homes and childhood influences with those having a lower sense of self-worth. He found three important characteristics which distinguished them: (1) The high-esteem children were clearly more loved and appreciated at home than were the low-esteem boys. (2) The high-esteem group came from homes where parents had been significantly more strict in their approach to discipline. By contrast, the parents of the low-esteem group had created insecurity and dependence by their permissiveness. Their children were more likely to feel that the rules were not enforced because no one cared enough to get involved. Furthermore, the most successful and independent young men during the latter period of the study were found to have come from homes that demanded the strictest accountability and responsibility. And as could have been predicted, the family ties remained the strongest, not only in the wishy-washy homes, but in the homes where discipline and self-control had been a way of life. (3) The homes of the high-esteem group were also characterized by democracy and openness. Once the boundaries for behavior were established, there was freedom for individual personalities to grow and develop. The boys could express themselves without fear of ridicule, and the overall atmosphere was marked by acceptance and emotional safety.[12]

I share your concern over the unjust emphasis on beauty and intelligence among children today. That's why we are playing down the importance of those two factors in our home. For ex-

ample, my son has very crooked teeth, but I tell him that it isn't important what he looks like. What matters is the person inside. Do you agree with this approach?

Not entirely. A parent who strongly opposes the unfortunate stress currently placed on beauty and brains, as I do, must resolve a difficult philosophical question with regard to his own children. While he recognizes the injustice of this value system, he knows his child is forced to compete in a world which worships those attributes. What should he do, then? Should he help his youngster become as attractive as possible? Should he encourage his "average" child to excel in school? Or would he be wise to de-emphasize these values at home, hoping the boy or girl will learn to live with his/her handicaps?

There are no "scientific" answers to those questions. I can only give you my considered opinion, in reply. Despite the injustice of this system, my child will not be the one to change it. I am obligated to help him compete in his world as best he can. If his ears protrude, I will have them flattened. If his teeth are crooked, I will see that they are straightened. If he flounders academically, I will seek tutorial assistance to pull him out. He and I are allies in his fight for survival, and I will not turn a deaf ear to his needs.

Rick Barry, the former professional basketball star, is a handsome, 6'7" specimen of health and confidence. Yet as a child he was humiliated and self-conscious about his teeth, even causing him to talk with his hand over his mouth. As he described in the book, *Confessions of a Basketball Gypsy*:

> When my second teeth came in, they came in crooked and two of them were missing in front. Maybe my folks could not afford to have them fixed, or maybe having teeth fixed was not then what it is now. I remember talking to Dad about putting in false teeth in front and wearing braces, which might cut my gums when I exerted myself playing ball. Anyway, I did not have my teeth fixed until I was in college. I was very sensitive about my teeth. I was ashamed to look at myself in the mirror. I used to keep my mouth shut and I'd never smile. I used to keep my hand over my mouth, which muffled my voice and made it hard for people to understand me. I developed

this habit of keeping my hand over my mouth, just sort of always resting on my chin, and I couldn't shake it for years afterward.

This kind of discomfort is incredibly painful to a child. That's why I believe it is a parental obligation, within the limits of financial resources, to eradicate the flaws which generate the greatest sensitivity. Dr. Edward Podolsky agrees. He is assistant supervisory psychiatrist at Kings County Hospital in New York City, and recommends that physical deformities be corrected before the child enters first grade, if possible. After that time, peer pressure becomes a major factor in shaping his self-concept.

But we parents must walk a tightrope at this point. While I am helping my child to compete in the world as it is, I must also teach him that its values are temporal and unworthy. Explaining the two contradictory roles of that coin requires considerable skill and tact. How can I urge my daughter to fix her hair neatly and then tell her, "Beauty doesn't matter?" The key is to begin very early to instruct the child on the true values of life: love for all mankind, kindness, integrity, trustworthiness, truthfulness, devotion to God, etc. Physical attractiveness is then described as part of a social game we must play. Since the world is our ball park, we cannot completely ignore the rules of the game. But whether we hit a home run or strike out, we can take comfort in knowing that baseball, itself, is not that important. Herein lies an anchor that can hold a child steady.[13]

What about good-natured teasing and joking within the family? Is it harmful to laugh and kid each other?

The most healthy families are those which can laugh together, and I certainly don't think our egos should be so fragile that we all have to walk on cracked eggs around each other. However, even innocent humor can be painful when one child is always the object of the jokes. When one youngster has an embarrassing feature, such as bed-wetting or thumb-sucking or stuttering or a striking physical flaw, the other members of the family should be encouraged to tread softly on the exposed nerves thereabout. And particularly, one should not ridicule a child for his size, whether he is a small boy or a large girl. There is nothing funny about that subject. This is the guiding principle: it is wise not to tease a child about the features he is also defending outside the home. And when he asks for any joke to end, his wishes should be honored.[14]

My twelve-year-old is embarrassed about the size of her nose. But what I can't understand is that she keeps talking about it to her friends. Should I call this to her attention and advise her *not* to mention this problem?

One of the most obvious characteristics of a person who feels inferior is that he talks about his deficiencies to anyone who will listen. An overweight person feels compelled to apologize to his companions for ordering a hot fudge sundae. He echoes what he imagines they're thinking: "I'm already fat enough without eating this," he says, scooping up the cherry and syrup with his spoon. Likewise, a woman who thinks she's unintelligent will admit freely, "I am really bad at math; I can hardly add two and two." This kind of self-denigration is not as uncommon as one might think.

While there is no virtue in becoming an image-conscious phony, trying to be something we're not, I believe it is also a mistake to go to the other extreme. While the person is blabbing about all of his ridiculous inadequacies, the listener is formulating a lasting impression of him.

So, I do recommend that you teach a "no-knock" policy to your daughter. She should learn that constant self-criticism can become a bad habit, and it accomplishes nothing. There is a big difference between accepting blame when it is valid and in simply chattering about one's inferiority. Your daughter should know that her friends are probably thinking about their *own* flaws, anyway.[15]

I want to get my six-year-old daughter ready for some of the esteem problems that will probably occur when she is a teenager. How can I begin bracing her for the social pressure she is likely to face?

In a sense, all of childhood is a preparation for adolescence and beyond. Mothers and fathers are granted a single decade to lay a foundation of values and attitudes that will help their children cope with the future pressures and problems of adulthood. As such, we would all do well to acquaint our young children with the meaning of self-worth and its preservation, since every human being has to deal with that issue at some point in the life cycle.

This teaching process should begin during the kindergarten years, if not before. For example, when your child meets someone who is too shy to speak or even look at him, you might say, "Why do you suppose Billie is too embarrassed to tell you what he is feeling? Do you think he doesn't have much self-confidence?" (Use the world *confidence* frequently, referring to a kind of courage and belief in one's self.) When your child participates in a school or church program, compliment him for having the confidence to stand in front of a group without hanging his head or thrusting his tongue in his cheek.

Then as the elementary years unfold, begin focusing on the negative side of that important ingredient. Talk openly about feelings of inferiority and what they mean. For example, "Did you notice how David acted so silly in class this morning? He was trying hard to make everyone pay attention to him, wasn't he? Do you have any idea why he needs to be noticed every minute of the day? Maybe it's because David doesn't like himself very much. I think he is trying to force people to like him because he thinks he is disrespected. Why don't you try to make friends with David and help him feel better about himself? Would you like to invite him to spend the night?"

Not only will you help your child "tune in" to the feelings of others through this instruction, but you will also be teaching him to understand his *own* feelings of inadequacy. Each year that passes should bring more explicit understandings about the crisis in worth which comes to everyone. It would be wise to give him an illustration of people who have overcome great feelings of inferiority (such as Eleanor Roosevelt), and ultimately, the *best* examples will come from the struggles of your own adolescent experiences. The goal is to send your pubescent son or daughter into the teen years, armed with four specific concepts: (1) all adolescents go through a time when they don't like themselves very much; (2) most feel ugly and dumb and unliked by their peer group; (3) the worst of this self-doubt will not last very long, although most human being have to deal with those feelings off and on throughout life; (4) each of us possesses incredible value because we are children of the Creator, who has a specific plan for our lives.

I suppose this strategy appeals to me, not only for its possible contribution to a healthy adolescence, but because it takes us in the direction of human understanding. And how badly that comprehension is needed! I read recently that 80 percent of the people who get fired from their jobs have not failed to perform as required. In other words, they do not lack *technical* skill or abilities. Their dismissal occurs because *they can't get along with people.* They misunderstand the motives of others and respond with belligerence and insubordination. We can minimize that possibility by training our children to "see" others in a truer light, while preserving their own dignity and sense of worth.[16]

I have heard that you are critical of the "Barbie" products and other teenage role-model dolls of this type. Explain the nature of your concern.

My objection to Barbie and her companions is on two levels. First, there could be no better method for teaching the worship of beauty and materialism than is done with these luscious dolls. If we intentionally sought to drill our babies on the necessity of growing up rich and gorgeous, we could do no better than has already been done. Did you ever see an ugly Barbie doll? Has she ever had even the slightest imperfection? Of course not! She oozes femininity and sex appeal. Her hair is thick and gleaming—loaded with "body" (whatever in the world that is). Her long, thin legs, curvaceous bust, and delicate feet are absolutely perfect. Her airbrushed skin is without flaw or blemish (except for a little statement on her bottom that she was "Made in Hong Kong"). She never gets pimples or blackheads, and there is not an ounce of fat on her pink body. Not only is Barbie one of the beautiful people, but so are all her buddies. Her swinging boyfriend, Ken, is an adolescent composite of Charles Atlas, Rock Hudson, and Clark Kent (mild-mannered reporter for the *Daily Planet*). These idealized models load an emotional time bomb set to explode the moment a real live thirteen-year-old takes her first long look in the mirror. No doubt about it—Barbie she ain't!

Yet it is not the physical perfection of these Barbie dolls (and her many competitors) that concerns me most; of much greater harm are the teenage games that they inspire. Instead of three-and four-year-old boys and girls playing with stuffed animals, balls, cars, trucks, model horses and the traditional memorabilia of childhood, they are now learning to fantasize about life as an adolescent. Ken and Barbie go on dates, learn to dance, drive sports cars, get suntans, take camping trips, exchange marriage vows, and have babies (hopefully in that order). The entire adolescent culture with its emphasis on sexual awareness is illustrated to tiny little girls who ought to be thinking about more childish things. This places our children on an unnatural timetable likely to reach the peak of sexual interest several years before it is due—with all the obvious implications for their social and emotional health.[17]

My child is often ridiculed and hurt by the other children on our block, and I don't know how to handle the situation. He gets very depressed and comes home crying frequently. How should I respond when this happens?

When your child has been rejected in this manner, he is badly in need of a friend—and you are elected. Let him talk. Don't try to tell him that it doesn't hurt or that it's silly to be so sensitive. Ask him if he knows what it is that his "friends" don't like. (He may be causing their reaction by dominance, selfishness, or dishonesty.) Be understanding and sympathetic without weeping in mutual despair. As soon as appropriate, involve yourself with him in a game or some other activity which he will enjoy. And finally, set about resolving the underlying cause.

I would suggest that you ask your child to invite one of his school friends to go to the zoo on Saturday (or offer other attractive "bait") and then spend the night at your house. Genuine friendship often grows from such beginnings. Even the hostile children on the block may be more kind when only one of them is invited at a time. Not only can you help your child make friends in this way, but you can observe the social mistakes he is making to drive them away. The information you gain can later be used to help him improve his relationship with others.[18]

My ten-year-old daughter hates to have her hair in a pigtail because her friends don't wear theirs that way. I have always loved pigtails, ever since I was a little girl. Am I wrong to make her please me by wearing her hair the way I want it?

Yes, particularly if your daughter feels unnecessarily different and foolish with her friends. Social pressure on the nonconformist is severe, and you should not place your daughter in this uncomfortable position. Closeness between generations comes from the child's knowledge that his parent understands and appreciates his feelings. Your inflexibility on this point reveals a lack of empathy and may bring later resentment.[19]

We have a four-year-old adopted child, and want to raise him to have a strong awareness of our love for him and of the love of God. What suggestions do you have for us and other parents of adopted children regarding the special needs that will arise?

The best answer I've found for that question quotes Dr. Milton I. Levine from the publication *Your Child from 2 to 5.*[20] I'll quote from that source and then comment on Dr. Levine's views.

*Common-Sense Approaches
to Adoption*
Adopting children has become such an accepted practice these days that the quavering question, "Shall I tell him he's adopted?" doesn't even qualify as soap-opera dialogue any more. Most parents realize that telling a youngster from the earliest possible moment

provides the only solid foundation for his and their security.

However, as Dr. Milton I. Levine, advisory board member of *2-to-5 World News* and Associate Professor of Pediatrics, New York Hospital— Cornell Medical Center, points out: "Even though adoption is no longer regarded as a shameful secret but rightly as a logical matter of fact, the situation still demands delicacy, understanding and many common-sense decisions on the part of parents."

Parents should tell the child about his adoption from the time he begins to beg for stories, says Dr. Levine. This will spare the youngster serious shock that can accompany the revelation in later years. Parents might treat the story as a wondrous chapter in the family's history. But the tendency to put off a decision sometimes affects even the best-intentioned adoptive parents. "Let's wait until he's old enough to understand," they may say, and delay the explanation until a basic fact turns into a dark secret. In Dr. Levine's opinion, even five- and six-year-olds are too old to be told without resultant emotional damage. He urges parents to:

1. Tell the child about his adoption from the moment he is ready to listen to stories.
2. Use the word "adopted" in the narrative until it becomes a synonym for "chosen" and "selected" and "wanted."
3. Make no attempt to conceal the adoption, even though moving into a new neighborhood might invite concealment.

"Some adoptive parents never seem to outgrow an apologetic attitude based on a feeling that they are merely pinch-hitting for the child's 'own' parents," says Dr. Levine. "For their own mental health, as well as their child's, they must accept the fact that they are, in reality, the youngster's parents. The mother and father who raise a child from infancy, giving him the love and care that enable him to grow freely, *are* the *real* parents; the strangers who produced the baby are merely *biological* parents. The difference can't be stressed strongly enough. By imparting to the child, even unconsciously, an unjustified feeling of loss—a feeling that he *had parents,* but now has substitutes, however loving—these adoptive parents endanger the child's security in his closest relationships and retard his understanding of the true role of parent."

Even professionals are divided over what to tell adopted children about their biological parents, Dr. Levine admits. There are at least three possible approaches, he points out, but not one can qualify as an answer:

1. Tell the child his biological parents are dead.
2. State plainly that the biological parents were unable to care for their baby themselves.
3. Tell the child nothing is known about the biological parents, but that he was secured from an agency dedicated to finding good homes for babies.

"There are pros and cons to all of these solutions," emphasizes Dr. Levine, who prefers the first approach because: "The child who is told that his biological parents are dead is free to love the mother and father he lives with. He won't be tormented by a haunting obligation to search for his biological parents when he's grown.

"Since the possibility of losing one's parents is one of childhood's greatest fears, it is true that the youngster who is told that his biological parents are dead may feel that all parents—including his second set—are pretty impermanent," concedes Dr. Levine. "Nevertheless, I feel that in the long run the child will find it easier to adjust to death than to abandonment. To tell a youngster that his parents gave him up because they were unable to take care of him is to present him with a complete rejection. He cannot comprehend the circumstances which might lead to such an act. But an unwholesome view of himself as an unwanted object, not worth fighting to keep, might be established.

Sex education is another thorny problem for adoptive parents. Any simple, natural explanation of reproduction stresses that a baby is conceived out of his mother's and father's love for each other and their desire to have a child. This explanation is reassuring to other children. But it may, because of the complexity of his situation, cause the adopted child to feel estranged from his adoptive parents, dubious about his own beginnings, and a little out of step with nature in general.

I would disagree with Dr. Levine only in reference to comments made about the biological parents. I am unwilling to lie to my child about anything, and would not tell him that his natural parents were dead if that were not true. Sooner or later, he will learn that he has been misled, which could bring the entire adoption story under suspicion.

Instead, I would be inclined to tell the child that very little is known about his biological parents. Several inoffensive and vague possibilities could be offered to him, such as, "We can only guess at the reasons the man and woman could not take care of a baby. They may have been extremely poor and unable to give you the care you needed; or perhaps the woman was sick; or she may not have had a home. We just don't know. But we *do* know that we're thankful that you could come be our son [or daughter], which was one of the greatest gifts God ever gave to us."

Furthermore, I would add three suggestions to Dr. Levine's comments. First, Christian parents should present the adoptive event as a tremendous blessing (as implied above) that brought great excitement to the household. Tell about praying for a child and waiting impatiently for God's answer. Then describe how the news came that the Lord had answered those prayers, and how the whole family thanked Him for His gift of love. Let your child know your delight when you first saw him lying in a crib, and how cute he looked in his blue blanket, etc. Tell him that his adoption was one of the happiest days of your life, and how you raced to the telephone to call all your friends and family members to share the fantastic news. (Again, I'm assuming that these details are true.) Tell him the story of Moses' adoption by Pharaoh's daughter, and how God chose him for a great work with the children of Israel. Look for other, similar illustrations which convey respect and dignity to the adoptee. You see, the child's interpretation of the adoptive event is almost totally dependent on the manner in which it is conveyed during the early years. Most certainly, one does not want to approach the subject sadly, admitting reluctantly that a dark and troublesome secret must now be confessed.

Second, celebrate *two* birthdays with equal gusto each year: the anniversary of his birth, and the anniversary of the day he became your son (or daughter). While other biological children in the family celebrate one birthday, the second hoopla will give the adopted child a compensative edge to offset any difference he might feel relative to his siblings. And use the word "adopted" openly and freely, until it loses its esoteric sting.

Third, when the foundation has been laid and the issue defused, then forget it. Don't constantly remind the child of his uniqueness to the point of foolishness. Mention the matter when it is appropriate, but don't reveal anxiety or tension by constantly throwing adoption in the child's face. Youngsters are amazingly perceptive at "reading" these thinly disguised attitudes.

I believe it is possible, by following these common sense suggestions, to raise an adopted child without psychological trauma or personal insult.[21]

You have been very critical of the value system in the Western world, which damages our self-concepts and mental health. What important changes could be made in our culture to produce a higher percentage of emotionally healthy children and adults?

In counseling with neurotic parents, it is apparent that emotional problems usually originate in one of two places (or both): either from an unloving or unnourishing relationship with parents, or from an inability to gain acceptance and respect from peers. In other words, most emotional disorders (except organic illness) can be traced to destructive relationships with people during the first twenty years of life.

Therefore, the most valuable revision would be for adults to begin actively teaching children to love and respect each other (and, of course, to demonstrate that love in their own lives).

Far from manifesting kindness and sensitivity, however, children are often permitted to be terribly brutal and destructive, especially to the handicapped child, the ugly child, the slow-learning child, the uncoordinated child, the foreign child, the minority child, the small or the large child, and the child who is perceived to be different from his peers in even the most insignificant feature. And predictably, the damage inflicted on young victims often reverberates for a lifetime.

Adults should devote their creative energies to the teaching of *love* and *dignity*. And, if necessary, we should *insist* that children approach each other with kindness. Can boys and girls be taught to respect their peers? They certainly can! Young people are naturally more sensitive and empathetic than adults. Their viciousness is a learned response, resulting from the highly competitive and hostile world which their leaders have permitted to develop. In short, children are destructive to the weak and lowly because we adults haven't bothered to teach them to "feel" for one another.

Perhaps an example will help explain my concern. A woman told me recently about her experience as a room mother for her daughter's fourth-grade class. She visited the classroom on Valentine's Day to assist the teacher with the traditional party on that holiday. Valentine's Day can be the most painful day of the year for an unpopular child. Every student *counts* the number of valentines he is given, as a direct measure of his social worth. This mother said the teacher announced that the class was going to play a game which required the formation of boy-girl teams. That was her first mistake, since fourth graders have not yet experienced the happy hormones which draw the sexes together. The moment the teacher instructed the students to select a partner, all the boys immediately laughed and pointed at the homeliest and least respected girl in the room. She was overweight, had protruding teeth, and was too withdrawn even to look anyone in the eye.

"Don't put us with Hazel," they all said in mock terror. "*Anybody* but Hazel! She'll give us a disease! Ugh! Spare us from Horrible Hazel." The mother waited for the teacher (a strong disciplinarian) to rush to the aid of the beleaguered little girl. But to her disappointment, nothing was said to the insulting boys. Instead, the teacher left Hazel to cope with that painful situation in solitude.

Ridicule by one's own sex is distressing, but rejection by the opposite sex is like taking a hatchet to the self-concept. What could this devastated child say in reply? How does an overweight fourth-grade girl defend herself against nine aggressive boys? What response could she make but to blush in mortification and slide foolishly into her chair? This child, whom God loves more than the possessions of the entire world, will never forget that moment (or the teacher who abandoned her in this time of need).

If I had been the teacher of Hazel's class on that fateful Valentine's Day, those mocking, joking boys would have had a fight on their hands. Of course, it would have been better if the embarrassment could have been prevented by discussing the feelings of others from the first day of school. But if the conflict occurred as described, with Hazel's ego suddenly shredded for everyone to see, I would have thrown the full weight of my authority and respect on her side of the battle.

My spontaneous response would have carried this general theme: "Wait just a minute! By what right do any of you boys say such mean, unkind things to Hazel? I want to know which of you is so perfect that the rest of us couldn't make fun of you in some way? I know you all very well. I know about your homes and your school records and some of your personal secrets. Would you like me to share them with the class, so we can all laugh at you the way you just did at Hazel? I could do it! I could make you want to crawl into a hole and disappear. But listen to me! You need not fear. I will *never* embarrass you in that way. Why not? Because it *hurts* to be laughed at by your friends. It hurts even more than a stubbed toe or a cut finger or a bee sting.

"I want to ask those of you who were having such a good time a few minutes ago: Have you ever had a group of children make fun of you in the same way? If you haven't, then brace yourself. Some day it will happen to you, too. Eventually you will say something foolish . . . and they'll point at you and laugh in your face. And when it happens, I want you to remember what happened today."

(*Then addressing the entire class.*) "Let's make sure that we learn something important from what took place here this afternoon. First, we will not be mean to each other in this class. We will laugh together when things are funny, but we will not do it by making one person feel bad. Second, I will *never* intentionally embarrass anyone in this class. You can count on that. Each of you is a child of God. He molded you with His loving hands, and He has said that we all have equal worth as human beings.

This means that Suzie is neither better nor worse than Charles or Mary or Brent. Sometimes I think maybe you believe a few of you are more important than others. It isn't true. Every one of you is priceless to God and each of you will live forever in eternity. That's how valuable you are. God loves every boy and girl in this room, and because of that, I love every one of you. He wants us to be kind to other people, and we're going to be practicing that kindness through the rest of the year."

When a strong, loving teacher comes to the aid of the least respected child in his class, as I've described, something dramatic occurs in the emotional climate of the room. Every child seems to utter an audible sigh of relief. The same thought is bouncing around in many little heads: "If Hazel is safe from ridicule—even overweight Hazel—then I must be safe, too." You see, by defending the least popular child in the room, a teacher is demonstrating (1) that he has no "pets"; (2) that he respects everyone; (3) that he will fight for anyone who is being treated unjustly. Those are three virtues which children value highly, and which contribute to mental health.

And may I suggest to parents, *defend the*

underdog in your neighborhood. Let it be known that you have the confidence to speak for the outcast. Explain this philosophy to your neighbors, and try to create an emotional harbor for the little children whose ship has been threatened by a storm of rejection. Don't be afraid to exercise *leadership* on behalf of a youngster who is being mauled. There is no more worthy investment of your time and energy.[22]

SECTION THREE
Parental Overprotection

Is it possible to love a child too much?

Not if the love is totally mature and unconditional. However, not everything that is called "love" is healthy for a child. Some Americans are excessively child-oriented at this stage in history; many parents have invested all of their hopes, dreams, desires, and ambitions in their youngsters. The natural culmination of this philosophy is overprotection of the next generation. I dealt with one anxious parent who stated that her children were the *only* sources of her satisfaction. During the long summers, she spent most of her time sitting at the front room window, watching her three girls while they played. She feared that they might get hurt or need her assistance, or they might ride their bikes in the street.

Her other home responsibilities were ignored, despite her husband's complaints. She did not have time to clean her house or cook meals; guard duty at the front window was her only function. She suffered enormous tension over the known and unknown threats that could hurt her beloved offspring.

Childhood illness and sudden danger are always difficult for a loving parent to tolerate, but the slightest threat produces unbearable anxiety for the overprotective mom and dad. Not only do they suffer; their child is often a victim, too.[1]

What happens to a child whose parents are overprotective and fail to assign appropriate responsibility to their child?

A dependency relationship may develop with far-reaching implications. Such a youngster often falls behind his normal timetable in preparation for ultimate release as a young adult. As a ten-year-old, he can't make himself do anything unpleasant, since he has never had any experience in handling the difficult. He does not know how to "give" to anyone else, for he has only thought of himself. He finds it hard to make decisions or exercise any kind of self-discipline. A few years later, he will steamroll into adolescence completely unprepared for the freedom and responsibility he will find there. And finally his future wife is in for some swell surprises which I shudder to contemplate.[2]

I want to avoid the dependency trap you described, but am not sure how it begins or how to head it off with an infant son. Alert me to the key elements in this process.

It is probably easier to foster an unhealthy dependency relationship between parent and child than it is to avoid one. Let's examine the mechanism as it often occurs. At the moment of birth, a little child is completely and totally helpless. One forgets just how dependent a newborn is—in fact, I want to forget it, just as soon as possible! That little creature lying in the crib can do nothing for himself: he doesn't roll over, he can't scratch his head, he is unable to verbalize his thoughts, and he won't lift a finger in his own behalf. Consequently, his parents are responsible for meeting his every need. They are his servants, and if they're too slow in meeting his demands, he is equipped with a spine-chilling scream to urge them into action. He bears no obligations whatsoever. He doesn't even have to appreciate their efforts. He won't say "please" or "thank you"; he doesn't apologize for getting them up six times in one night; he even offers no sympathy when at 3:01 A.M. his exhausted mom drives the point of a safety pin through the fleshy part of her thumb (without doubt, the greatest agony in human experience!). In other words, a child begins his life in a state of complete and total dependence on those whose name he bears.

About twenty years later, however, at the other end of childhood, we expect some radical changes to have occurred in that individual. He should then be able to assume the full responsibilities of young adulthood. He is expected to spend his money wisely, hold down a job, be loyal to one woman, support the needs of his family, obey the laws of the land, and be a good citizen. In other words, during the course of childhood, an individual should progress from a position of *no* responsibility to a position of full responsibility. Now, how does little John-John get from position A to position B? How does this magical transformation of self-discipline take place? There are many self-appointed experts on child raising who seem to feel it all should happen toward the latter end of adolescence, about fifteen minutes before Big John leaves home permanently. Prior to that time, he should be allowed to do whatever he wishes at the moment.

I reject that notion categorically. The best preparation for responsible adulthood is derived from training in responsibility during childhood. This is not to say that the child should be forced to act like an adult. It does mean that he can be encouraged to progress on an orderly timetable of events, carrying the level of responsibility that is appropriate for his age. Shortly after birth, for example, the mother begins transferring responsibilities from her shoulders to those of her infant. Little by little he learns to sleep through the night, hold his own bottle, and reach for what he wants. Later he is potty-trained (hopefully), and he learns to walk and talk. Gradually, as each new skill is mastered, his mother "frees" herself that much more from this servitude.

Each year he should make more of his own decisions than in the prior twelve months; the routine responsibilities of living should fall to his shoulders as he is able to handle them. A seven-year-old, for example, is usually capable of selecting his own clothing for the day. He should be keeping his room straight and making his bed each morning. A nine- or ten-year-old may be carrying more freedom, such as in the choice of television programs to watch (within reason). I am not suggesting that we abdicate parental leadership altogether; rather, I believe we should give conscious thought to the reasonable, orderly transfer of freedom and responsibility, so that we are preparing the child each year for that moment of full independence which must come.[3]

You wrote in one of your books, "All of life is a preparation for adolescence and beyond." Please explain and elaborate on that statement.

I was referring, again, to this need to grant independence to children and permit them to make their own decisions. Parents would be wise to remember that the day is fast approaching when the child they have raised will pack his suitcase and leave home, never to return. And as he walks through the door to confront the outside world, he will no longer be accountable to their parental authority and supervision. He can do what he chooses. No one can require him to eat properly, or get his needed rest, or find a job, or live responsi-

bly, or serve God. He will sink or swim on
his own.

This sudden independence can be devastating for some individuals who have not
been properly prepared for it. But how can
a mother and father train sons and daughters so that they won't go wild in the first
dizzying months of freedom? How can they
equip them for that moment of emancipation?

The best time to begin preparing a child
for the ultimate release is during
toddlerhood, before a relationship of dependence is established. As Renshaw
wrote:

> It may be messier for the child to feed
> himself; more untidy for him to dress
> himself; less clean when he attempts
> to bathe himself; less perfect for him
> to comb his hair; but unless his
> mother learns to sit on her hands and
> allow the child to cry and to try, she
> will overdo for the child, and indepen-
> dence will be delayed.[4]

This process of granting appropriate independence must continue through the elementary school years. Parents should
permit their kids to go to summer camp

even though it might be "safer" to keep them at home. Likewise, boys and girls ought to be allowed to spend the night with their friends when invited. They should make their own beds, take care of their animals, and do their homework. When this assignment has been handled properly through the years, a high school senior should be virtually emancipated, even though he still lives with his parents.[5]

My mother waited on me hand and foot when I as a child and I would feel guilty if I didn't serve the needs of my kids as well. Do you really think it is in their best interest for me to do less for them?

I'm not suggesting that you give up mothering and nurturing your children, but it *is* appropriate for you to let them carry the level of responsibility that their age and maturity permits. This point was made by Marguerite and Willard Beecher, writing in their excellent book, *Parents on the Run.* They stated, and I strongly agree, that *the parent must gain his freedom from the child, so that the child can gain his freedom from the parent.* Think about that for a moment. If you never get free from your child by transferring responsibility to him, then he remains hopelessly bound to you, too! You have knotted each other in a paralyzing interdependency which stifles growth and development.

I admit the difficulty of implementing this policy. Our deep love for our children makes us tremendously vulnerable to their needs. Life inevitably brings pain and sorrow to little people, and we hurt when they hurt. When others ridicule them or laugh at them, when they feel lonely and rejected, when they fail at something important, when they cry in the midnight hours, when physical harm threatens their existence—these are the trials which seem unbearable to those of us who watch from the sidelines. We want to rise like a mighty shield to protect them from life's sting—to hold them snugly within the safety of our embrace. Yet there are times when we must let them struggle. Children can't grow without taking risks. Toddlers can't walk initially without falling down. Students can't learn without facing some hardships. And ultimately, an adolescent can't enter young adulthood until we release him from our protective custody.[6]

Why is it difficult for mothers, especially, to grant this independence and freedom to their kids?

There are several reasons for the reluctance to let go. I've observed that the most common motivation reflects the unconscious emotional needs of the mother. Perhaps the romance has gone out of her marriage, leaving the child as the only real source of affection. Maybe she has trouble making lasting friendships. For whatever reason, she wants to be the "heavy" in the life of her child. Thus, she becomes his servant. She refuses to obtain her freedom from him for the specific purpose of denying him his. I know one mother-daughter team which maintained this interlocutory relationship until the mother's death at ninety-four years of age. The daughter, then seventy-two, found herself unmarried, alone, and on her own for the first time in her life. It's a frightening thing to endure in old age what other people experienced in adolescence.

I recently counselled another mother whose husband had died when their only son, Davie, was a baby. She had been left with the terrifying task of raising this lad by herself, and Davie was the only person left in the world whom she really loved. Her reaction was to smother him totally. The boy was seven years of age when she came to me. He was afraid to sleep in a room by himself. He refused to stay with a baby-sitter, and he even resisted going to school. He did not dress himself and his behavior was infantile in every regard. In fact, instead of waiting in the reception room while I talked to his mother, he found my office and stood with his hand on the doorknob for an hour, whimpering and begging to be admitted. His mother interpreted all of this as evidence of his fear that she would die, as his father had done. In response, she bound him even more tightly to her, sacrificing all her own needs and desires: she could neither go on dates nor bring any men into their home; she could not get involved in any activities of her own or have any adult experiences without her cling-along son. You see, she had never gained her freedom from Davie, and in turn, Davie had not gained his freedom from his lovin' momma.[7]

I sense that this task of letting go is one of the most important responsibilities parents face.

You are right. If I were to list the five most critical objectives of parenting, this one would rest near the top: "Hold them close and let them go." Parents should be deeply involved in the lives of their young children, providing love and protection and authority. But when those children reach their late teens and early twenties, the cage door must be opened to the world outside. That is the most frightening time of parenthood, particularly for Christian mothers and fathers who care so deeply about the spiritual welfare of their families. How difficult it is to await an answer to the question, "Did I train them properly?" The tendency is to retain control in order to avoid hearing the wrong reply to that all-important question. Nevertheless, our sons and daughters are more likely to make proper choices when they do not have to rebel against our meddling interference.

Let me emphasize the point by offering another phrase which could easily have been one of King Solomon's Proverbs, although it does not appear in the Bible. It states, "If you love something, set it free. If it comes back to you, then it's yours. If it doesn't return, then it never was yours in the first place." This little statement contains great wisdom. It reminds me of a day last year when a wild coyote pup trotted in front of my house. He had strayed into our residential area from the nearby mountains. I managed to chase him into our backyard where I trapped him in a corner.

After fifteen or twenty minutes of effort, I succeeded in placing a collar and leash around his neck. He fought the noose with all his strength, jumping, diving, gnawing, and straining at the tether.

Finally, in exhaustion, he submitted to his servitude. He was my captive, to the delight of the neighborhood children. I kept the little rascal for an entire day and considered trying to make a pet of him. However, I contacted an authority on coyotes, who told me the chances were very slim that I could tame his wild streak. Obviously, I could have kept him chained or caged, but he would never really have belonged to me. Thus, I asked a game warden to return the lop-eared creature to his native territory in the canyons above Los Angeles. You see, his "friendship" meant nothing to me unless I could set him free and he would remain with me by his own choice.

My point is that love demands freedom. It is true not only of relationships between animals and man, but also in all human interactions. For example, the quickest way to destroy a romantic love between a husband and wife is for one partner to clamp a steel cage around the other. I've seen hundreds of women trying unsuccessfully to demand love and fidelity from their husbands. It won't work. Think back to your dating experiences before marriage. Do you recall that romantic relationships were doomed the moment one partner began to worry about losing the other, phoning six or eight times a day and hiding behind trees to see who was competing for the lover's attention? That hand wringing performance will devastate a perfectly good love affair in a matter of days. To repeat, *love demands freedom.*

Why else did God give us the choice of either serving Him or rejecting His companionship? Why did He give Adam and Eve the option of eating forbidden fruit in the Garden of Eden, instead of forcing their obedience? Why didn't He just make men and woman His slaves who were programmed to worship at His feet? The answers are found in the meaning of love. God gave us a free choice because there is no significance to love that knows no alternative. It is only when we come to Him because we hungrily seek His fellowship and communion that the relationship has any validity. Isn't this the meaning of Proverbs 8:17, whereby He says, "I love them that love me; and those that seek me early shall find me" (KJV)? That is the love that only freedom can produce. It cannot be demanded or coerced or required or programmed against our will. It can only be the product of a free choice which is honored even by the Almighty.

The application of this perspective to older adolescents (especially those in their early twenties) should be obvious. There comes a point where our record as parents is in the books, our training has been completed, and the moment of release has arrived. As I did with the young coyote, we must unsnap the leash and remove the collar. If our "child" runs, he runs. If he marries the wrong person, he marries the wrong person. If he takes drugs, he takes drugs. If he goes to the wrong school, or rejects his faith, or refuses to work, or squanders his inheritance on liquor and prostitutes, then he must be permitted to make these destructive choices and take the consequences of those decisions.

In summary, let me say that adolescence is not an easy time of life for either generation; in fact, it can be downright terrifying. But the key to surviving this emotional experience is to lay the proper foundation and then face it with courage. Even the inevitable rebellion of the teen years can be a healthy factor. This conflict contributes to

the process by which an individual changes
from a dependent child to a mature adult,
taking his place as a co-equal with his parents. Without that friction, the relationship
could continue to be an unhealthy
"mommie-daddy-child" triad, late into adult
life, with serious implications for future
marital harmony. If the strain between generations were not part of the divine plan of
human development, it would not be so universally prevalent, even in homes where
love and authority have been maintained in
proper balance.[8]

**The following question was posed by
Family Life Today, a Christian magazine devoted to family issues and interests: What do you do when your
child, at age eighteen or twenty,
makes choices quite different from
what you had hoped? Parents feel
frustrated and embarrassed—at a loss
to influence the child they thought
had been "trained up in the way he
should go" but who is now "departing
from it." Parenting begins when a
child is born. But does it ever end?
Should it? If so, when? And how?**

My answer reprinted below is used by
permission of *Family Life Today* magazine

(Copyright 1982), and was originally published in the March 1982 issue.

"The process of letting go of our offspring should begin shortly after birth and conclude some twenty years later with the final release and emancipation," said Dobson, who readily admits this is the most difficult assignment parents face. "The release is not a sudden event. In fact, from infancy onward, the parent should do nothing for the child that the child can profit from doing for himself. Refusal to grant appropriate independence and freedom results in rebellion and immaturity—whether during the terrible twos or later in adolescence."

A strong advocate of loving discipline during the early years, Dobson contends that there comes a time when the relationship between generations must change. "By the time a child is eighteen or twenty," he noted, "the parent should begin to relate to his or her offspring more as a peer. This liberates the parent from the responsibility of leadership and the child from the obligation of dependency.

"It is especially difficult for us *Christian* parents to release our children into adulthood because we care so much about the outcome of our training. Fear of rebellion and rejection of our values and beliefs often leads us to retain our authority until it is torn from our grasp. By then, permanent damage may have been done to family relationship."

One of the most difficult times for parents to remain reserved is when their young adult offspring chooses a mate not to the parents' liking. "Though it is painful to permit what you think would be a marital mistake," Dobson warned, "it is unwise to become dictatorial and authoritarian in the matter. If you set yourself against the person your child has chosen to marry, you may struggle with in-law problems the rest of your life.

"If there are well-grounded reasons for opposing a potential marriage, a parent can be honest about those convictions at an opportune moment and in an appropriate manner. But that does not entitle the older generation to badger and nag and criticize those who are trying to make this vitally important decision."

For example, he suggested that in such a situation a parent might say: "I have great concern about what you're doing and I'm going to express my views to you. Then I'll step aside and allow you to make up your own mind. Here are the areas of incompatibility that I foresee (etc.) . . . I'm going to be praying for you as you seek the Lord's will in this important matter." The most critical ingredient, Dobson concluded, is to make it clear that the decision is "owned" by the offspring— not the parent.

What are the consequences of not handling these crises properly? "Unresolved conflicts during late adolescence have a way of continuing into the adult years," replied Dobson. A recent mail-in survey he conducted revealed that 89 percent of the 2,600 people responding felt that they suffered from long-term strained relationships with their own parents. Forty-four percent complained specifically that their parents had never set them free or granted them adult status.

And, added Dobson, the letters that

accompanied the survey responses told incredible stories—of a twenty-three-year-old girl who was regularly spanked for misbehavior and others in mid-life who still did not feel accepted and respected by their parents. "Clearly," he said, "the process of letting go is a very difficult process for *most* parents."

What can a mother or father do if the offspring has gone into openly sinful behavior that violates everything the parent has stood for? And how should they react, for example, when their grown kids forsake family ties and join a "New Age" religious group?

"I have not recommended that parents keep their concerns and opinions to themselves," said Dobson, "especially when eternal issues hang in the balance. There is a time to speak up. But the manner in which the message is conveyed must make it clear that the parents' role is advisory . . . not authoritarian. The ultimate goal is for parents to assure the young person of their continued love and commitment, while speaking directly about the dangers that are perceived. And I repeat, it must be obvious that the responsibility for decision-making ultimately rests with the offspring."

Dobson, whose books on family interaction have dominated the "top ten" Christian best-seller lists for many months, mused that his next book will probably be about guilt in parenthood. Referring to Proverbs 22:6, he said he agrees with Dr. John White that the Proverbs are presented as *probabilities,* not *promises:* "Even if we train up a child in the way he should go, he *sometimes* goes his own way! That's why we parents tend to experience tremendous guilt that is often unjustified. Our kids live in a sinful world and they often emulate their peers; despite our teaching to the contrary. God gives each child a free will and He will not take it from them—nor can we."

Citing several environmental and inborn factors that parents do not control—including individual temperament, peer-group pressures and the innate will of the child—Dobson noted that these combined forces are probably more influential than parental leadership itself. "It is simply unfair to attribute everything young adults do . . . good or bad . . . to parental skill or ignorance.

"A hundred years ago when a child went wrong, he was written off as a 'bad kid.' Now, any failure or rebellion in the younger generation is blamed on the parents—supposedly reflecting their mistakes and shortcomings. Such a notion is often unjust and fails to acknowledge a young adult's freedom to run his own life."

What attitude, then, should a parent have toward a twenty-one-year-old offspring who insists on living with someone of the opposite sex? "It is difficult to force anything on a person that age, and in fact, a parent shouldn't try," Dobson warned. "But Mom and Dad certainly do not have to pay for the folly."

He noted that the father of the Prodigal Son, symbolizing God's patient love, permitted his son to enter a life of sin. But he didn't send his servants to "bail out" his erring youngest when times got difficult.

"It was the son's choice to go into a sinful life-style, and the father permitted both the behavior and the consequences," Dobson observed. "An overprotective parent who continually sends money to an irresponsible offspring, often breaks this necessary connection between sinful behavior and painful consequences.

"A parent's goal should be to build a friendship with his or her child from the cradle onward," Dobson concluded. "When his task is done properly, both generations can enjoy a lifetime of fellowship after the child has left home and established a family of his own."

After talking with this noted Christian psychologist, one leaves with the impression that parents who once looked with awe and wonder at their bundle of new life may find the delivery of that same child into adulthood two decades later no less a marvel. And just as they could not keep their newborn child in the safety and protection of the womb, they must ultimately permit his or her passage into the grown-up world at the end of childhood. Along the way, wise Christian parents will prayerfully try to influence—but not prolong control over—their maturing child. The rest they leave in the hands of the Creator.

SECTION FOUR
Self-Esteem in Adulthood

If I understand your writings correctly, you believe a majority of Americans experience low self-esteem to one degree or another. Assuming that to be true, what are the *collective* implications of that poor self-concept?

It has serious implications for the stability of the American culture because the health of an entire society depends on the ease with which its individual members can gain personal acceptance. Thus, whenever the keys to self-esteem are seemingly out of reach for a large percentage of the people, as in twentieth-century America, then widespread mental illness, neuroticism, hatred, alcoholism, drug abuse, violence, and social disorder will certainly occur. Personal worth is not something human beings are free to take or leave. We must have it, and when it is unattainable, everybody suffers.[1]

Why do you think low self-esteem is so widespread among women today? Why is this problem more prevalent now than in the past?

There appear to be three factors related to the epidemic of self-doubt among females at this time in our history. First, the traditional responsibilities of wives and mothers have become matters of disrespect and ridicule. Raising children and maintaining a home hold very little status in most areas of the country, and women who are cast into that role often look at themselves with unconcealed disenchantment.

The forces which have promulgated this viewpoint are everywhere at once—on television, in magazines, on radio, in newspapers, in written advertisements, in books and novels—each one hacking steadily at the confidence and satisfaction of women at home. It is not surprising, then, that many American homemakers feel bypassed . . . disrespected by the society around them. They would have to be deaf and blind to have missed that message.

But the decline in self-respect among women has other causes, as well. Another highly significant factor has to do with the role of beauty in our society. Physical attractiveness (or the lack of it) has a profound impact on feminine self-esteem. It is very difficult to separate basic human worth from the quality of one's own body; therefore, a woman who feels ugly is almost certain to feel inferior to her peers. This pressure is greatly magnified in a highly eroticized society as ours. Isn't it reasonable that the more steamed up a culture becomes over sex (and ours is at the boiling point), the more likely it is to reward beauty and punish ugliness? When sex becomes super-significant as it is today, then those with the least sex appeal necessarily begin to worry about their inability to compete in that marketplace. They are bankrupt in the most valuable "currency" of the day. Millions have fallen into that trap.

A third source of low self-esteem among American women relates to basic intelligence. Simply stated, many feel dumb and stupid. Psychologists have known for decades that there is no fundamental difference in the overall level of intelligence between men and women, although there are areas of greater strength for each sex. Men tend to score higher on tests of mathematics and abstract reasoning, while women excel in language and all verbal skills. However, when the individual abilities are combined, neither sex has a clear advantage over the other. Despite this fact, women are much more inclined to doubt their own mental capacity than are men. Why? I don't know, but it is another very important factor in low self-esteem.[2]

Then you are saying that low self-esteem among women is still greatly influenced by the same physical factors they worried about when they were younger?

That's right. The importance of beauty does not end in adolescence. It continues to determine human worth to some degree until late in life. Let me give you an example of what I mean. I counseled a young woman who had been a beautiful airline stewardess a few years earlier. She was happily married to a man who was proud of her beauty. Then a most unfortunate thing happened. She was in a tragic automobile accident which scarred her face and twisted her body. Her back was broken and she was destined to walk with a cane for the rest of her life. She was no longer attractive and her husband quickly lost interest in her sexually. Their divorce followed shortly. As a cripple, she could no longer serve as a stewardess, of course, and she found it difficult to obtain a job of any type. In this instance, a girl with high personal worth plunged to a position of little social status in one brief moment. Her true value as a human being should not have been affected by her accident, but it certainly was in the eyes of her immature husband.

While there are many causes for low self-esteem among women today, that old nemesis called "the uglies" (which every woman experiences at least occasionally) keeps doing its dirty work throughout our society.[3]

Are the influences of "beauty" and "brains" as important to adult males as females? How does the self-esteem of men differ from women in this regard?

For men, physical attractiveness gradually submerges as a value during late adolescence and early adulthood, yielding first place to intelligence. For women, however, beauty retains its number-one position throughout life, even into middle age and beyond. *The reason the average woman would rather have beauty than brains is because she knows the average man can see better than he can think.* Her value system is based on his and will probably continue that way. A man's personal preferences are also rooted in the opinions of the opposite sex, since most women value intelligence over handsomeness in men.[4]

My husband often makes fun of my body. He's just teasing, but his comments embarrass me and make me disinterested in sex. Why can't I just ignore his kidding, because I know he doesn't mean to hurt me?

Sex for human beings is inseparably connected with our psychological nature, especially in women. A woman who feels ugly, for example, is often too ashamed of her imperfect body to participate in sex without embarrassment. She knows it is impossible to disguise forty-year-old thighs, and her flaws interfere with her sensuality. Likewise, the person who feels shy and timid and inferior will usually express his sexuality in similar terms, or on the other hand, a self-confident, emotionally healthy individual is more likely to have a spontaneous sex life.

You must teach this concept to your husband, if possible, helping him see that anything which reduces your self-esteem will probably be translated into bedroom problems. In fact, any disrespect which he reveals for you as a person is almost certain to crop up in your physical relationship. In this regard, our sexual behavior differs radically from the mechanistic responses of lower animals. The emotional concomitants simply cannot be denied or suppressed in human beings.[5]

I have never felt beautiful or even attractive to the opposite sex. Does this explain why I am *extremely* modest, even being ashamed to be seen in a bathing suit?

Modesty has three basic origins. First, it is built into our fallen human nature. After sinning in the Garden of Eden, Adam and Eve's eyes "were opened, and they knew that they were naked; and they sewed fig leaves together, and made themselves aprons" (Gen. 3:7 KJV). To a varying degree within the descendants of Adam, we have inherited this same sensitivity about our bodies.

Second, modesty is a product of early home life. Those who were taught to conceal themselves compulsively in front of other family members usually carry that excessive modesty even into their marital relationships. It can turn legitimate sexual experiences into a self-conscious obligation.

The third source of extreme modesty is the one you mentioned, and it is probably the most powerful. Those who are ashamed of their bodies are highly motivated to conceal them. One of the greatest fears among junior high students is that they will have to disrobe and shower in front of their peers. Boys and girls alike are terrified by the possibility of ridicule for their lack of development (or precociousness). This embarrassment is often retained in the adult years with feelings of inferiority stamped all over it.[6]

What part does intelligence play in the self-esteem of *adults?* Do they tend to forget the trouble they had during the school years?

It has been said that "a boy is the father of the man," meaning we grown-ups are direct products of our own childhood. Thus, everything I have written about self-esteem in children applies to adults as well. We are all graduates of the educational "fail factory," and few have escaped completely unscathed. Furthermore, our self-worth is *still* being evaluated on the basis of intelligence. Dr. Richard Herrnstein, a Harvard University psychologist, predicts that a caste system founded on IQ is coming to America. He believes people will soon be locked into rigid intellectual classes which will determine careers, earning power, and social status. Dr. Herrnstein's expectation is based on the disintegration of racial and sexual barriers to success, leaving only intelligence as the major remaining source of discrimination in America. I don't agree fully with Dr. Herrnstein, although I am certain we will see the continuing importance of mental ability to self-esteem in our technological world.[7]

My sister struggles with feelings of low self-esteem much of the time. I have a hard time understanding what she is experiencing. Can you put into words what a person goes through when they feel inadequate and inferior?

I will try to express the troubling thoughts and anxieties which reverberate through the backroads of an insecure mind. It is sitting alone in a house during the quiet afternoon hours, wondering why the phone doesn't ring . . . wondering why you have no "real" friends. It is longing for someone to talk to, soul to soul, but knowing there is no such person worthy of your trust. It is feeling that "they wouldn't like me if they knew the real me." It is becoming terrified when speaking to a group of your peers, and feeling like a fool when you get home. It is wondering why other people have so much more talent and ability than you do. It is feeling incredibly ugly and sexually unattractive. It is admitting that you have become a failure as a wife and mother. It is disliking everything about yourself and wishing, constantly wishing, you could be someone else. It is feeling unloved and unlovable and lonely and sad. It is lying in bed after the family is asleep, pondering the vast emptiness inside and longing for unconditional love. It is intense self-pity. And more than any other factor, it is the root cause of depression.[8]

I have a friend who was married for nine years before her husband left her for another woman. I think she was a loving and devoted wife, yet she

seemed to feel that the break-up of her marriage was her own fault. As a result, her self-esteem disintegrated and has never recovered. Why would she blame herself when her husband lied and deceived her and ran off with a younger girl?

It has always been surprising for me to observe how often the wounded marriage partner—the person who was clearly the victim of the other's irresponsibility—is the one who suffers the greatest pangs of guilt and feelings of inferiority. How strange that the one who tried to hold things together in the face of obvious rejection often finds herself wondering, "How did I fail him? . . . I just wasn't woman enough to hold my man . . . I am 'nothing' or he wouldn't have left . . . If only I had been more exciting as a sexual partner . . . I drove him to it . . . I wasn't pretty enough . . . I didn't deserve him in the first place."

The blame for marital disintegration is seldom the fault of the husband or the wife alone. It takes two to tango, as they say, and there is always some measure of shared blame for a divorce. However, when one marriage partner makes up his mind to behave irresponsibly, to become involved extramaritally, or to run from his family commitments and obligations, he usually seeks to justify his behavior by magnifying the failure of his spouse. "You didn't meet my needs, so I had to satisfy them somewhere else," is a familiar accusation. By increasing the guilt of his partner in this way, he reduces his own culpability. For a husband or wife with low self-esteem, these charges and recriminations are accepted as fact when hurled his way. "Yes, it was my fault. I drove you to it!" Thus, the victim assumes the full responsibility for his partner's irresponsibility, and self-worth shatters.

I would not recommend that your friend sit around hating the memory of her husband. Bitterness and resentment are emotional cancers that rot us from within. However, if I were counseling her I would encourage her to examine the facts carefully. Answers to these questions should be sought: "Despite my human frailties, did I value my marriage and try to preserve it? Did my husband decide to destroy it and then seek justification for his actions? Was I given a fair chance to resolve the areas of greatest irritation? Could I have held him even if I had made all the changes he wanted? Is it reasonable that I should hate myself for this thing that has happened?"

Your friend should know that social rejection breeds feelings of inferiority and self-pity in enormous proportions. And rejection by the one you love, particularly, is *the* most powerful destroyer of self-esteem in the entire realm of human experience. She might be helped to see herself as a victim of this process, rather than a worthless failure at the game of love.[9]

I am acquainted with a woman who needs people so badly, but she unintentionally drives them away. She talks too much and constantly complains and makes everyone want to run from her. I know she has a terrible inferiority complex, but I could help her if she would let me. How can I tell her about these irritating faults without making her feel even worse about herself?

You do it the way porcupines make love: *very,* very carefully. Let me offer a general principle that has thousands of applications in dealing with people, including the situation you have posed. *The right to criticize must be earned, even if the advice is constructive in nature.* Before you are entitled to tinker with another person's self-esteem, you are obligated *first* to demonstrate your own respect for him as a person. This is accomplished through an atmosphere of love and kindness and human warmth. Then when a relationship of confidence has been carefully constructed, you will have earned the right to discuss a potentially threatening topic. Your motives have thereby been clarified.

In response to your specific question, I would suggest that you invest some effort in building a healthy relationship with your verbose friend, and then feed her suggestions in very small doses. And remember all the while that someone, somewhere, would like to straighten out a few of your flaws, too. We all have them.[10]

I have suffered from low self-esteem for years, and sought help from a psychiatrist during a particularly depressed period of my life. Rather than building my self-worth, however, he was cold and aloof with me. I had the feeling he was merely doing a job and never really cared about me. I wonder how *you* would approach a patient with my kind of problem.

It has been discouraging for me to see how often my professional colleagues (psychiatrists, psychologists, and counselors) have overlooked the feelings you described as a most obvious root cause for emotional distress. Lack of self-esteem produces more symptoms of psychiatric disorders than any other factor yet identified.

Time and time again in my casework as a psychologist, I sit talking to a person with deep longings to be respected and accepted. How badly he needs human affection and kindness, as well as emotional support and suggestions for change. Yet if that same needy patient had gone to Dr. Sigmund Freud in his day, the immortal grandfather of psychoanalysis would have sat back in detached professionalism, analyzing the patient's sexual repressions. If a patient had sought treatment from Dr. Arthur Janov, originator of Primal Scream therapy, he would have been encouraged to roll on the floor and bawl like a baby. (How foolish that form of "therapy" appears from my perspective!) Other modern therapists would have required the same patient to assault and be assaulted by other members of an "encounter group," or remove his clothing in a group, or beat his mother and father with a belt. Believe it or not, one of the major areas of controversy at psychiatric conferences a few years ago involved the wisdom of female patients having sexual intercourse with their male therapists!

Have we gone completely mad? Whenever men abandon their ethics, they cease to make sense, regardless of their professional degrees and licenses. Perhaps this is why psychiatry is called "the study of the id by the odd." (No disparagement is intended to the more orthodox profession of psychiatry itself.)

The most successful approach to therapy for a broken patient, I firmly believe, is to convey the following message with conviction (though perhaps not with words): "Life has been tough and you have become acquainted with pain. To this point, you've faced your problems without much human support, and there have been times when your despair has been overwhelming. Let me, now, share that burden. From this moment forward, I am interested in you as a person; you deserve and shall have my respect. As best as possible, I want you to quit worrying about your troubles. Instead, confide them to me. Our concentration will be on the present and the future; together we will seek appropriate solutions."

Suddenly, the beleaguered patient no longer feels alone—the most depressing of human experiences. "Someone cares! Someone understands! Someone assures me with professional confidence that he is certain I will survive. I'm not going to drown in that sea of despondence, as I feared. I have been thrown a life preserver by a friend who promises not to abandon me in the storm." This is real therapy, and it exemplifies the essence of the Christian commandment that we "bear one another's burdens."[11]

I am *not* coping so well with the problems of self-doubt. I feel ugly and disrespected and unworthy. What encouragement can you offer?

Isn't it about time that you made friends with yourself? Aren't there enough headaches in life without beating your skull against that old brick wall of inadequacy, year after year? If I were to draw a caricature that would symbolize the millions of adults like you with low self-esteem, I would depict a bowed, weary traveler. Over his shoulder I would place the end of a mile-long chain to which is attached tons of scrap iron, old tires, and garbage of all types. Each piece of junk is inscribed with the details of some humiliation—a failure—an embarrassment—a rejection from the past. He could let go of the chain and free himself from that heavy load which immobilizes and exhausts him, but he is somehow convinced that it must be dragged throughout life. So he plods onward, digging a furrow in the good earth as he goes.

You can free yourself from the weight of the chain if you will but turn it loose. Your inferiority is based on a distortion of reality seen through childish eyes. The standards by which you have assessed yourself are themselves changing and fickle. Dr. Maxwell Maltz, the plastic surgeon who authored *Psycho-Cybernetics,* said women came to him in the 1920s requesting that their breasts be reduced in size. Today they are asking that he pump them up with silicone. False values! In King Solomon's biblical love song, his bride asked him to overlook her dark skin that had occurred from exposure to the sun. In his day, right meant white. But now Solomon's bronze wife would be the pride of the beach. False values! Modern women are ashamed to admit that they carry an extra ten pounds of weight, yet Rembrandt would have loved to paint their plump, rotund bodies. False values! Don't you see that your personal worth is not really dependent on the opinions of others and the temporal, fluctuating values they represent? The sooner you can accept the transcending worth of your humanness, the sooner you can come to terms with yourself. I must agree with the writer who said: "While in the race to save our face, why not conquer inner space?" It's not a bad idea.[12]

I am dealing with my own inadequacies pretty well, and now feel I am ready to take additional steps in the direction of self-confidence. What do you recommend?

I could take a week to answer this question, but let me just offer the first suggestion that comes to mind. I have repeatedly observed that a person's own needs and problems seem less threatening when he is busy helping someone else handle theirs! It is difficult to concentrate on your own troubles when you are actively shouldering another person's load and seeking solutions to his problems. Therefore, I would recommend that you consciously make a practice of giving to others. Visit the sick. Bake something for your neighbors. Use your car for those without transportation. And perhaps most important, learn to be a good listener. The world is filled with lonely, disheartened people like you were, and you are in an excellent position to empathize with them. And while you're doing it, I guarantee that your own sense of uselessness will begin to fade.[13]

You might also enjoy reading the book by Dr. W. Peter Blitchington, *The Christian Woman's Search for Self-Esteem* (Thomas Nelson, Inc., 1982), which provides many helpful suggestions.

You are strongly in favor of building self-esteem in children, but I have some theological problems with that objective. The Bible condemns "pride" from Genesis to Revelation, and speaks of humans as no better than worms. How do you defend your position in the light of Scripture?

It is my opinion that great confusion has prevailed among followers of Christ on the distinction between pride and self-esteem. You are apparently among the people who actually believe that Christians should maintain an attitude of inferiority in order to avoid the pitfalls of self-sufficiency and haughtiness. I don't believe it.

After speaking to a sizable audience in Boston a few years ago, I was approached by an elderly lady who questioned my views. I had discussed the importance of self-confidence in children, and my comments had contradicted her theology. In fact, she even made reference to the same Scripture in Psalm 22:6.

She said, "God wants me to think of myself as being no better than a worm."

"I would like to respect myself," she continued, "but God could not approve of that kind of pride, could He?"

I was touched as this sincere little lady spoke. She told me she had been a missionary for forty years, even refusing to marry in order to serve God more completely. While on the foreign field, she had become ill with an exotic disease which now reduced her frail body to ninety-five pounds. As she spoke, I could sense the great love of the Heavenly Father for this faithful servant. She had literally given her life in His work, yet she did not even feel entitled to reflect on a job well done during her closing years on earth.

Unfortunately, this fragile missionary (and thousands of other Christians) had been taught that she was worthless. But that teaching did not come from the Scriptures. Jesus did not leave His throne in heaven to die for the "worms" of the world. His sacrifice was intended for that little woman, and for me and all of His followers, whom He is not embarrassed to call brothers. What a concept! If Jesus is now my brother, then that puts me in the family of God, and guarantees that I will outlive the universe itself. And that, friends, is what I call genuine self-esteem!

It's true that the Bible clearly condemns the concept of human pride. In fact, God apparently holds a special hatred for this particular sin. I have counted 112 references in Scripture which specifically warn against an attitude of pride. Proverbs 6:16-19 makes is unmistakably clear:

> These six things doth the Lord hate: yea, seven are an abomination unto him: A proud look, a lying tongue, and hands that shed innocent blood, an heart that deviseth wicked imaginations, feet that be swift in running to mischief, a false witness that speaketh lies, and he that soweth discord among brethren (KJV).

Isn't it interesting that a *proud look* (or *haughtiness,* as paraphrased in *The Living Bible*) is listed *first* among God's seven most despised sins, apparently outranking adultery, profanity, and other acts of disobedience? Anything given that prominence in the Word had better be avoided scrupulously by those wishing to please the Lord. But first we must interpret the meaning of the word *pride*.

Language is dynamic and the meaning of words changes with the passage of time. In this instance, the word *pride* has many connotations today which are different from the biblical usage of the word. For example, a parent feels "pride" when his son or daughter succeeds in school or wins a race. But I can't believe the Lord would be displeased by a father glowing with affection when he thinks of the boy or girl entrusted to his care.

We speak, also, about the "Pride of the Yankees," or a person taking pride in his work, or the pride of a southern cook. These are very positive emotions that mean the individual is dedicated to his craft, that he has self-confidence, and that he will deliver what he promises. Certainly those attitudes could not represent the pinnacle of the seven deadliest sins.

I'm equally convinced that the Bible does not condemn an attitude of quiet selfrespect and dignity. Jesus commanded us to love our neighbors *as* ourselves, implying not only that we are permitted a reasonable expression of self-love, but that love for others is impossible—until we experience a measure of self-respect.

Then what *is* the biblical meaning of pride? I believe sinful pride occurs when our arrogant self-sufficiency leads us to violate the two most basic commandments of Jesus: first, to love God with all our heart, mind, and strength; and second, to love our neighbor as ourselves. A proud person is too pompous and haughty to bow humbly before his Maker, confessing his sins and submitting himself to a life of service to God; or he is hateful to his fellowman, disregarding the feelings and needs of others. And as such, most of the ills of the world, including war and crime, can be laid at its door. That's why the writer of Proverbs put "a proud look" above all other evils, for that is where it belongs.

May I stress, further, that the quest for self-esteem *can* take us in the direction of unacceptable pride. During the past decade, for example, we've seen the rise of the "Me" generation, nurtured carefully by humanistic psychologists, who accept no scriptural dictates. One of the best-selling books of this era was entitled *Looking Out for #1,* which instructed its readers to grab the best for themselves. Widely quoted mottos reflect the same selfish orientation, including *if it feels good, do it!* and *do your own thing*. This philosophy of "me first" has the power to blow our world to pieces, whether applied to marriage, business, or international politics.

In summary, I have not recommended a philosophy of Meism. I have not suggested that children be taught arrogance and self-sufficiency or that they be lured into self-ishness. (That will occur without any encouragement from parents.) My purpose has been to help mothers and fathers preserve an inner physical, mental, and spiritual health. And I believe that objective is in harmony with biblical perspectives.[14]

SECTION FIVE
Depression in Women

Is depression more common among men or women?

Depression occurs less frequently in men and is apparently more *crisis*-oriented. In other words, men get depressed over specific problems such as a business setback or an illness. However, they are less likely to experience the vague, generalized, almost indefinable feeling of discouragement which many women encounter on a regular basis. Even a cloudy day may be enough to bring on a physical and emotional slow-down, known as the blahs, for those who are particularly vulnerable to depression.[1]

When women get depressed, what specific complaint or irritant is most commonly related to the condition?

I have asked that question of more than 10,000 women who were given an opportunity to fill out a questionnaire entitled, "Sources of Depression in Women." At the top of the list was the problem of low self-esteem. More than 50 percent of an initial test group marked this item above every other alternative on the list, and 80 percent placed it in the top five. This finding is perfectly consistent with my own observations and expectations: even in seemingly healthy and happily married young women, self-doubt cuts the deepest and leaves the most wicked scars. This same old nemesis is usually revealed within the first five minutes of a counseling session; feelings of inadequacy and lack of confidence have become a way of life for millions of American women.[2]

My wife has been severely depressed for nearly three months. What kind of treatment or therapy would you recommend for her?

Get her to a physician, probably an internist, as soon as possible. This kind of prolonged depression can have serious medical and psychological consequences, yet it is usually very responsive to treatment. Antidepressant drugs are highly effective in controlling most cases of severe depression. Of course, the medication will not correct the circumstances which precipitated her original problem, and the possibility of low self-esteem and the other causes must be faced and dealt with, perhaps with the help of a psychologist or psychiatrist.[3]

I tend to feel depressed after every holiday, but I don't know why. These special days are very happy ones for my family. Why do I find myself "blue" after such enjoyable occasions?

It will be helpful for you to understand the nature of emotional rhythm in human beings. Anything producing an extreme "high" will set the stage for a later "low," and vice versa. A few years ago, for example, my wife and I bought a newer home. We had waited several years to find the right house, and we became very excited when escrow closed and the property was finally ours. The elation lasted for several days, during which time I discussed the experience with Shirley. I mentioned that we had been very high and that our excitement could not continue indefinitely. Emotions don't operate at maximum velocity for very long. More important, it was likely that our mental set would drop below sea level within a very short period of time. As expected, we both experienced a vague letdown into mild depression about three days later. The house didn't seem so wonderful and there wasn't anything worth much enthusiasm. However, having anticipated the "downer," we recognized and accepted its temporary fluctuation when it came.

Depression therefore should be understood as a relatively predictable occurrence. It is likely to appear, as in your case, following a busy holiday or after the birth of a baby, a job promotion, or even after a restful vacation. The cause for this phenomenon is partly physical in nature. Elation consumes greater quantities of body energy, since all systems are operating at an accelerated rate. The necessary consequence of this pace is fatigue and exhaustion, bringing with it a more depressed state. Thus, highs *must* be followed by lows. The system is governed by a psychological law. You can depend on it. But in the healthy individual, fortunately, lows eventually give way to highs, too.[4]

We live in what you have described as "routine panic" in our home. I have

**three children under six, and I never
get caught up with my work. How can
I slow down when it takes every minute of the day (and night) to care for
my children?**

There may be a helpful answer in the
way you spend your money. Most Americans maintain a "priority list" of things to
purchase when enough money has been
saved for that purpose. It is my conviction
that domestic help for the mother of small
children should appear on that priority
list. Without it, she is sentenced to the
same responsibility day in and day out,
seven days a week. For several years, she
is unable to escape the unending burden of
dirty diapers, runny noses, and unwashed
dishes. She will do a more efficient job in
those tasks and be a better mother if she
can share the load with someone else occasionally. This seems more important to the
happiness of the home than buying new
drapes or a power saw for Dad.

But how can middle-class families afford
housecleaning and baby sitting services in
these inflationary days? It might be accomplished by using competent high school
students instead of older adults. I suggest
that a call be placed to the counseling office
of the nearest senior high school. Tell the

counselor that you need a mature third- or fourth-year student to do some cleaning. Do not reveal that you're looking for a regular employee. When the referred girl arrives, try her out for a day and see how she handles responsibility. If she's very efficient, offer her a weekly job. If she is slow and flighty, thank her for coming and call for another student the following week. There is a remarkable difference in maturity level between high school girls, and you'll eventually find one who works like an adult.

Here are some further suggestions to help you tolerate the pressures of your life:

1. Reserve some time for yourself. At least once a week, go bowling or shopping, or simply "waste" an occasional afternoon. In addition, a husband and wife should have a date every week or two, leaving the children at home, and even forgetting them for an evening.

2. Don't struggle with things you can't change. Concentrate on the good things in your life. Men and women should recognize that discontent can become nothing more than a bad habit—a costly attitude that can rob them of the pleasure of living.

3. Don't deal with any big problems late at night. All problems seem more unsolv-

able in the evenings, and the decisions that are reached then may be more emotional than rational.

4. Try making a list. The advantages of writing down one's responsibilities are threefold: (1) You know you aren't going to forget anything. (2) You can guarantee that the most important jobs will get done first. Thus, if you don't get finished by the end of the day, you will at least have done the items that were most critical. (3) The tasks are crossed off the list as they are completed, leaving a record of what has been accomplished. 5. Seek divine assistance. The concepts of marriage and parenthood were not human inventions. God, in His infinite wisdom, created and ordained the family as the basic unit of procreation and companionship. The solutions to the problems of modern parenthood can be found through the power of prayer and personal appeal to the Great Creator.[5]

My wife is a full-time homemaker, and we have three children under six years of age. She often gets depressed, especially when she can't keep up with everything expected of her. But I have my hands too full and am required to put in so much overtime.

What can I do to help Marge cope with these busy years?

Let me make two suggestions to you:

1. For some reason, human beings (and particularly women) tolerate stresses and pressures much more easily if at least one other person knows they are enduring it. This principle is filed under the category of "human understanding," and it is highly relevant to homemakers. The frustrations of raising small children and handling domestic duties will be more manageable for your wife if you will let her know that you comprehend it all. Even if you can do nothing to change the situation, simply your awareness that Marge did an admirable job today will make it easier for her to repeat the assignment tomorrow. Instead, the opposite usually occurs. At least eight million husbands will stumble into the same unforgivable question tonight: "What did you do all day, dear?" The very nature of the question implies that the little woman had been sitting on her back-side watching television and drinking coffee since arising at noon! The little woman could kill him for saying it.,

Everyone needs to know that he is respected for the way he meets his responsibilities. Husbands get this emotional nurture through job promotions, raises in pay, annual evaluations, and incidental praise during the work day. Women at home get it from their husbands—if they get it at all. The most unhappy wives and mothers are often those who handle their fatigue and time pressure in solitude, and their men are never very sure why they always act so tired.

2. Husbands *and* wives should constantly guard against the scourge of overcommitment. Even worthwhile and enjoyable activities become damaging when they consume the last ounce of energy or the remaining free moments in the day. Though it is rarely possible for a busy family, everyone needs to waste some time every now and then— to walk along kicking rocks and thinking pleasant thoughts. Men need time to putter in the garage and women need to pluck their eyebrows and do the girlish things again. But as I have described, the whole world seems to conspire against such reconstructive activities. Even our vacations are hectic, "We have to reach St. Louis by sundown or we'll lose our reservations."

I can provide a simple prescription for a happier, healthier life, but it must be implemented by the individual family. *You*

must resolve to slow your pace; you must
learn to say "no" gracefully; you must resist
the temptation to chase after more plea-
sures, more hobbies, more social entangle-
ments; you must "hold the line" with the
tenacity of a tackle for a professional football team. In essence, three questions
should be asked about every new activity
which presents itself: Is it worthy of our
time? What will be eliminated if it is
added? What will be its impact on our family life? My suspicion is that most of the
items in our busy day would score rather
poorly on this three-item test.[6]

**I notice that spiritual discouragement
and defeat are much more common
when I am tired than when I am
rested. Is this characteristic of others?**

When a person is exhausted, he is attacked by ideas he thought he conquered
long ago. The great football coach for the
Green Bay Packers, Vince Lombardi, once
told his team why he pushed them so hard
toward proper physical conditioning. He
said, "Fatigue makes cowards of us all." He
was absolutely right. As the reserves of
human energy are depleted, one's ability to
reject distressing thoughts and wild impressions is greatly reduced.[7]

I am depressed much of the time and worry about whether or not my kids will be affected by my moods. Are children typically vulnerable to parental discouragement and depression?

According to Dr. Norman S. Brandes, child psychiatrist, children are *very* sensitive to depression in the adults around them. They often become depressed themselves, even though adults think they've hidden their despair from the children. Furthermore, you are being watched carefully by your children and they are "learning" how to deal with frustration. In short, you are effectively teaching them, through your own depression, to react similarly in the future.

If your depression continues to be chronic, as you indicated, I would suggest that you seek professional advice. Begin with your physician, who may recognize a physical cause for your constant discouragement. If not, he may refer you for psychological assistance. This does not mean you are mentally ill or neurotic. It may indicate nothing more than that you need to examine the things that are bothering you with the help of a competent counselor.[8]

Can you explain why so many Americans express a dissatisfaction with life, despite the fact that we have more of the world's good things than any other country? It seems strange that the richest country on earth is inhabited by a high percentage of depressed and unhappy people.

The human emotional apparatus is constructed so as to disregard that which is taken for granted. Good health, delicious food, pleasant entertainment, peaceful circumstances, and beautiful homes are of little consequence to those who have had them since birth. Can you recall seeing a healthy teenager get up in the morning and express appreciation because his joints didn't hurt, or his vision was excellent, or because he breathed with ease or he felt so good? Not likely. He has never known the meaning of prolonged pain or sickness, and he accepts his good health without even considering it. But when those greatest of life's blessings begin to vanish, our appreciation for them increases accordingly. For a man who faces continued physical deterioration and premature death, the whole world assumes new significance: the beauty of a tree, the privilege of watching a sunset, the company of loved ones—it all takes on meaning.

I think this concept explains many of the emotional problems and psychiatric symptoms which beset us. We have been taught to anticipate the finest and best from our existence on this earth. We feel almost entitled, by divine decree, to at least seventy-two years of bliss, and anything less than that is a cause for great agitation. In other words, our *level of expectations* is incredibly high. But life rarely delivers on that promise. It deals us disappointment and frustration and disease and pain and loneliness, even in the best of circumstances. Thus, there is an inevitable gap between life as it *is* and life as it ought to be.

The result is a high incidence of depression, especially among women, an unacceptable rate of suicide, especially among the young, and a general anxiety among the rest of us. I have watched men develop ulcers over relatively insignificant business reverses. I have seen women suffer daily agitation over the most minor inconveniences, such as having a ragged couch or a cranky neighbor, when every other dimension of their lives was without blemish.

Compare the instability of such individuals with the attitudes of German families near the close of World War II. Every day, a thousand British bombers unloaded their destructive cargo over Hamburg and Berlin and Munich. By night, the American planes did the same. Loved ones were dying on all sides. Neighborhoods were shattered and burned. Little children were maimed and killed. There was not enough food to eat and the water was polluted. The fabric of their lives was shredded. Yet historians tell us that their morale remained intact until the end of the war. They did not crack. They went about the business of reordering their homes and making the best of a horrible situation.

How can we account for this courage in the face of disaster, as compared with affluent Americans who, though they have everything, are wringing their hands in the offices of psychiatrists? The difference can be found in our level of expectations. The Germans expected to sacrifice and experience suffering. They were, therefore, prepared for the worst when it came. But we are vulnerable to the slightest frustration, because we have been taught that troubles can be avoided. We have permitted our emotions to rule us, and in so doing, we have become mere slaves to our feelings.[9]

SECTION SIX

Understanding Premenstrual Tension

Is the moodiness I feel before my menstrual periods something that all women suffer? I feel as if I am some kind of freak because I get so depressed and touchy each month.

You are definitely not a freak! What you are experiencing is suffered by at least 30 percent of American women each month. There are many symptoms that characterize premenstrual tension, including sluggishness, irritability, lack of energy, hostility, low level of tolerance to noise, low self-esteem, depression, insecurity, low libido (sex drive), and a vague apprehension about the future.[1]

Describe in greater detail the mood fluctuations that are associated with the menstrual cycle each month. Is it true that this chemical influence is evident not only during or before a period, but at other times also?

It has been said, quite accurately, that the four weeks of the menstrual cycle can be characterized by the four seasons of the year. The first week after a period can be termed the springtime of the physiological calendar. New estrogens (female hormones) are released each day and a woman's body begins to rebound from the recent winter.

The second week represents the summertime of the cycle, when the living is easy. A woman during this phase has more self-confidence than during any other phase of the month. It is a time of maximum energy, enthusiasm, amiability, and self-esteem. Estrogen levels account for much of this optimism, reaching a peak during mid-cycle when ovulation occurs. The relationship between husband and wife is typically at its best during these days of summer, when sexual drive (and the potential for pregnancy) are paramount.

But alas, fall must surely follow summer.

Estrogen levels steadily dwindle as the woman's body prepares itself for another period of menstruation. A second hormone called progesterone is released, which reduces the effect of estrogen and initiates the symptoms of premenstrual tension. It is a bleak phase of the month. Self-esteem deteriorates day by day, bringing depression and pessimism with it. A bloated and sluggish feeling often produces not only discomfort but also the belief that "I am ugly." Irritability and aggression become increasingly evident as the week progresses, reaching a climax immediately prior to menstruation. Then come the winter and the period of the menstrual flow.

Women differ remarkably in intensity of these symptoms, but most experience some discomfort. Those most vulnerable even find it necessary to spend a day or two in bed during the "winter" season, suffering from cramping and generalized misery. Gradually, the siege passes and the refreshing newness of springtime returns.[2]

I've noticed that I experience the greatest feeling of inadequacy and inferiority during the "premenstrual" phase, a few days before my period.

Can you explain why this would be true?

Few women know that there is direct relationship between estrogen levels (the primary female sex hormones) and self-esteem. Thus, self-worth typically fluctuates predictably through the twenty-eight-day cycle. The graph which appears below depicts this relationship.

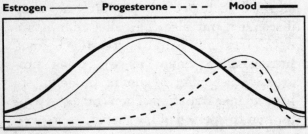

Estrogen ——— Progesterone – – – – Mood ▬▬▬▬

MENSTRUATION   MIDCYCLE   PREMENSTRUATION

Normal Hormone Levels and Mood. In the normal menstrual cycle, estrogen peaks at midcycle (ovulation). Both estrogen and progesterone circulate during the second half of the cycle, falling off rapidly just prior to menstruation. Moods change with the fluctuating hormone levels: women feel the greatest self-esteem, and the least anxiety and hostility, at midcycle.

Notice that estrogen levels are at their lowest point during menstruation (at the left of the graph), as is the general "mood."

The production of estrogen increases day by day until it peaks near the time of ovulation at midcycle. That midpoint also happens to be the time of greatest emotional optimism and self-confidence. Then another hormone, progesterone, is produced during the second half of the cycle, bringing with it increasing tension, anxiety, and aggressiveness. Finally, the two hormones decrease during the premenstrual period, reducing the mood to its lowest point again.[3]

How do we know that the symptoms of premenstrual tension are not merely psychological; perhaps women feel bad each month because they expect (or have been conditioned) to be miserable.

In the first place menstrual difficulties are seen in women around the world in vastly different cultures. Furthermore, the effect of premenstrual tension is not only observable clinically, but it can be documented statistically.

The incidence of suicides, homicides, and infanticides perpetrated by women are significantly higher during the period of premenstrual tension than any other phase of the month. Consider also the findings of

Alec Coppen and Neil Kessel, who studied 465 women and observed that they were more irritable and depressed during the premenstrual phase than during midcycle.

This was true for neurotic, psychotic, and normal women alike. Similarly, Natalie Sharness found the premenstrual phase associated with feelings of helplessness, anxiety, hostility, and yearning for love. At menstruation, this tension and irritability eased, but depression often accompanied the relief, and lingered until estrogen increased.[4]

Thousands of studies have validated this same conclusion. If you doubt their findings, ask a woman.[5]

Even though I know my depression is the result of physiological conditions each month, I still forget that fact and find myself suffering from low self-esteem and general anxiety. How can I prepare myself to do a better job of coping with the menstrual cycle?

It is impossible to prepare yourself for premenstrual tension unless you know what to expect, so you need to begin by conducting some research on your own body. I suggest that you keep a diary on which you describe at least three elements of your functioning: (1) your energy level, (2) your general mood, and (3) your achievements and accomplishments. Chart these three indicators *every day* for at least four months. Most women report that a surprisingly consistent pattern exists from month to month. Once it is identified and understood, further steps can be taken to brace yourself for the predictable valleys and tunnels.

Once the period of premenstrual tension arrives, you should interpret your feelings with caution and skepticism. If you can remember that the despair and sense of worthlessness are hormonally induced and have nothing to do with reality, you can withstand the psychological nosedive more easily. You should have a little talk with yourself each month, saying: "Even though I feel inadequate and inferior, I refuse to believe it. I know I'll feel differently in a few days and it is ridiculous to let this get me down. Though the sky looks dark, my perception is distorted. My real problem is physical, not emotional, and it will soon improve!"[6]

I don't think my husband understands the problems I experience during the menstrual cycle. Will you offer some advice to him about these physiological factors?

Having never had a period, it is difficult for a man to comprehend the bloated, sluggish feeling which motivates the wife's snappy remarks and irritability during the premenstrual period.

I am reminded of an incident related to me by my late friend Dr. David Hernandez, who was an obstetrician and gynecologist in private practice. The true story involves Latin men whose wives were given birth control pills by a pharmaceutical company. The Federal Drug Administration in America would not permit hormonal research to be conducted, so the company selected a small fishing village in South America which agreed to cooperate. All the women in the town were given the pill on the same date, and after three weeks the prescription was terminated to permit menstruation. That meant, of course, that every adult female in the community was experiencing premenstrual tension at the same time. The men couldn't take it. They all headed for their boats each month and remained at sea until the crisis passed at home.

Going fishing is not the answer to monthly physiological stresses, of course. It is extremely important for a man to learn to anticipate his wife's menstrual period, recognizing the emotional changes which will probably accompany it. Of particular importance is the need for affection and tenderness during this time, even though she may be rather unlovable for three or four days. He should also avoid discussions of financial problems or other threatening topics until the internal storm has passed, and keep the home atmosphere as tranquil as possible. He might even give his wife the speech described in the previous answer.

Let me conclude by addressing a final comment directly to husbands, expanding on the advice offered above. Because stress is such an influential factor in this problem of premenstrual tension, anything you can do to reduce environmental pressure is sure to help her feel better. If you are aware of the times when she is going to be feeling the strain, you should lighten the family commitments. Eating out can reduce the obligation to plan and cook meals. Do what you can to keep the kids out of her hair, especially the noisy younger ones. Take them to the park for an afternoon. Read to them or engage them in a quiet game, leaving their mother free to relax as much as possible.

Because your wife's sexual desire is at a low ebb that week, make fewer physical demands on her—but continue to be affectionate, reassuring, and loving toward her. Remember that women often feel "ugly" when they are experiencing premenstrual tension, so let her know that you find her as attractive as ever.

In some ways, the husband's role during his wife's menstrual period should be that of an understanding, loving, gentle parent. Just as parents do more giving than receiving, this is a man's time to support his wife in every way possible.[7]

Why are some women more prone than others to have unpleasant symptoms at the crucial time of the month?

Some good answers to this question are supplied by an excellent booklet entitled *Premenstrual Blues,* written by a California physician, Dr. Guy Abraham. He has kindly given me permission to refer to information in that booklet, although the following items are not direct quotations.

Dr. Abraham pinpoints six factors which

may make some women particularly prone to premenstrual tension:

1. Marriage. Married women are more susceptible than single women. In fact, premenstrual tension has been identified as a major cause of divorce.

2. Childbirth. The more pregnancies a woman has had, the more likely she is to experience the distressing symptoms associated with the days preceding menstruation.

3. Age. The premenstrual syndrome appears to become more and more acute during the childbearing years, up to the late thirties.

4. Stress. Time pressure and psychological tension contribute significantly to the problem.

5. Diet. Poor nutrition is a culprit here, including the excessive use of refined sugars and salt in the diet.

6. Exercise. Women who suffer from premenstrual tension are usually those who do not engage in regular outdoor exercise such as walking, bicycling, swimming, tennis, and other such activities.[8]

You mentioned the role of nutrition in the severity of premenstrual tension. Can I really help relieve the symptoms

by eating right? If so, what should my diet consist of?

I am firmly convinced of the importance of good nutrition . . . this is true for everyone of course, but especially for women during the childbearing years. And yes, a proper diet *is* related to the symptoms of premenstrual stress. One of the most uncomfortable symptoms of PMT (premenstrual tension), for example, is the bloated feeling a woman gets from having excess fluid in her body. This can be relieved by ingesting a low-salt diet, thus avoiding the retention of fluids. Of further help is restricting carbohydrates, especially sugar, and eating more protein. This may require considerable discipline, because there seems to be an unusual craving for sweets at this time—especially for chocolate. You should also increase the intake of vitamin C and the B complex vitamins, either in pill form or by eating more of the foods which contain these vitamins.

Regular exercise will also prove to be an asset to your health and well-being. Be sure to include some walking, bicycling, jogging, swimming, golfing, or other activity in your schedule every day.[9]

Is PMT similar to menopause in emotional characteristics?

In the sense that estrogen levels are reduced during both phases, yes. Since self-esteem is apparently related to estrogen, for example, a woman's feelings of low self-esteem are evident both premenstrually and during menopause. It has also been hypothesized that women who experience severe emotional fluctuations during their periods are more likely to experience some degree of menopausal distress in years to come. In other words, the vulnerability to estrogen is demonstrated early in life and confirmed during the middle-age years.[10]

When my wife is suffering from PMT, she not only becomes irritable and short-tempered, but she seems to become even more angry when I try to tell her everything will be all right and that it isn't as bad as it seems. How do you explain that?

You are observing the same lesson that I had to learn in my earlier counseling experience. I remember one patient in particular who used to call me or visit my office every twenty-eight days without exception. She was always tremendously depressed and agitated, but she never seemed to realize that her despair was related to her hormonal calendar. I would explain to her that she wasn't really so bad off, and things would be much better in a few days. To my surprise, however, these attempts to console her only caused greater frustrations and made her try to prove to me how terrible things were in her life. After thinking about her plight for a while, I realized that she had not come to me for answers, but for the assurance that one other human being on earth understood what she was going through.

After that, when this woman came to see me, I offered her empathy and understanding, helping her express the frustrations bottled up within. She would weep for forty or fifty minutes, telling me that there was no hope at all, and then blow her nose and sniff and say, "Thank you for your help. I feel so much better and I don't know what I would have done without you to talk to today." All I had done was let her know I understood. That was enough.

I suspect that your wife wants the same reassurance. There are times when we could *all* use a dose of that medicine.[11]

Since "the pill" is actually composed of estrogen, do women who take it

fluctuate emotionally as you have described?

It depends on the kind of pill prescribed. If estrogen and progestin (synthetic progesterone) are given *simultaneously* for twenty days and then ceased, the mood remains at a moderately low level and is characterized by mild anxiety throughout the month. However, if estrogen is given for fifteen days and estrogen-progestin for five, the mood fluctuation is very similar to the normal non-pill cycle. Your physician can provide more information as to your particular pill and its emotional reverberations.[12]

SECTION SEVEN

A Christian Perspective on Anger

The Bible condemns the emotion of anger, and yet Christians and non-Christians experience it. How can we be expected to remove this most common human response from our personalities?

Before we conclude that we cannot do what the Scriptures require, we must be sure we understand the context. Remember that words change their meaning with the passage of time. Just as the word "prido" has many meanings, so too has "anger" become a sort of "catch-all" phrase. Many of the behaviors which had been included under the definition of anger may have nothing to do with scriptural condemnation. Consider these examples:

1. Extreme fatigue produces a response which has the earmarks of anger. A mother who is exhausted from the day's activities can become very "angry" when her four-year-old spills his third glass of milk. This mother might give her life for her child if required, and she would not harm a hair on his fuzzy little head. Nevertheless, her exhausted state of distress is given the same generalized label as the urge which caused Cain to kill Abel. There is no relationship between the two distinct emotions represented.

2. Extreme embarrassment typically produces a reaction which is categorized under the same overworked heading.

3. Extreme frustration gives rise to an emotional response which we also call anger. I have seen this reaction from a high school basketball player, for example, who had an "off night" when everything went wrong. Perhaps he fumbled the ball away and double-dribbled and missed all his shots at the basket. The more he tried, the worse he played and the more foolish he felt. Such frustrations can trigger a volcanic emotional discharge at the coach or anyone in his way. Such are the irritations

which cause golf clubs to be wrapped around trees and tennis rackets to be impaled on net-posts.

4. Rejection is another occurrence which often generates a kind of angry response. A girl who is jilted by the boy she loves, for example, may retaliate with a flurry of harsh words. Far from hating him, however, her response is motivated by the deep hurt associated with being thrown over—discarded—disrespected.

You see, anger has come to represent many strong, negative feelings in a human being. Accordingly, I doubt if all the Scriptures which address themselves to the subject of anger are referring equally to the entire range of emotions under that broad category.[1]

Is all anger sinful?

Obviously, not everything that can be identified under the heading of anger is a violation of God's law, for Ephesians 4:26 instructs us to be "be angry, and sin not." That verse says to me that there is a difference between *strong feeling,* and the seething hostility which is consistently condemned in Scripture. Our first task, it would appear, is to clarify that distinction.[2]

Is it possible to prevent all feelings of anger?

No. It's important to remember that anger is not only emotional—it is biochemical, as well. The human body is equipped with an automatic defensive system, called the "flight or fight" mechanism, which prepares the entire organism for action. Adrenalin is pumped into the bloodstream which sets off a series of physiological responses within the body. Blood pressure is increased in accordance with an acceleration in heartbeat; the eyes are dilated for better peripheral vision; the hands get sweaty and the mouth becomes dry; and the muscles are supplied with a sudden burst of energy. In a matter of seconds, the individual is transformed from a quiet condition to an "alarm reaction state." *Most important, this is an involuntary response which occurs whether or not we will it.*

Once the flight or fight hormones are released, it is impossible to ignore the intense feelings they precipitate. It would be like denying the existence of a toothache or any other tumultuous physical occurrence. And since God created this system as a means by which the body can protect itself against danger, I do not believe He condemns us for its proper functioning.

On the other hand, our *reaction* to the feeling of anger is more deliberate and responsive to voluntary control. When we sullenly "replay" the agitating event over and over in our minds, grinding our teeth in hostility and seeking opportunities for revenge, or lash out in some overt act of violence, then it is logical to assume that we cross over the line into sinfulness. If this interpretation of the Scripture is accurate, then the exercise of the *will* stands in the gap between the two halves of the verse "be angry," . . . "and sin not."[3]

But doesn't the Bible take an absolute position on the subject of anger? Where does it allow for the individual differences you described?

Didn't the Apostle Paul write in Romans 12:18, "As much as lieth in you, live peaceably with all men"? In other words, we are all expected to exercise self-control and restraint, but some will be more successful than others by the nature of the individual temperaments. While we are at different levels of maturity and responsibility, the Holy Spirit gently leads each of us in the direction He requires, until a moment of truth arrives when He demands our obedience.[4]

All right, you have made it clear that some reactions which are called "anger" are involuntary and appear not to be condemned by God. Now flip that coin over. Under what circumstances is anger sinful, in your opinion?

I see unacceptable anger as that which motivates us to hurt our fellowman—when we want to slash and cut and inflict pain on another person. Remember the experience of the Apostle Peter when Jesus was being crucified? His emotions were obviously in a state of turmoil, seeing his beloved Master being subjected to an unthinkable horror. However, Jesus rebuked him when he severed the Roman soldier's ear with a sword. If there ever was a person with an "excuse" to lash out in anger, Peter seemed to be justified; nevertheless, Jesus did not accept his behavior and He compassionately healed the wounded soldier.

There is a vitally important message for all of us in this recorded event. *Nothing* justifies an attitude of hatred or a desire to harm another person, and we are treading on dangerous ground when our thoughts and actions begin leading us in that direction. Not even the defense of Jesus Christ would justify that kind of aggression.[5]

Are you saying that being "right" on an issue does not purify a wrong attitude or behavior?

Yes. In fact, having been in the church all my life, I've observed that Christians are often in greater danger when they are "right" in a conflict than when they are clearly wrong. In other words, a person is more likely to become bitter and deeply hostile when someone has cheated him or taken advantage of him than is the offender himself. E. Stanley Jones agreed, stating that a Christian is more likely to sin by his reactions than his actions. Perhaps this is one reason why Jesus told us to "turn the other cheek" and "go the second mile," knowing that Satan can make devastating use of anger in an innocent victim.[6]

If anger is unquestionably sinful when it leads us to hurt another person, then is the evil only involved in the aggressive act itself? What if we become greatly hostile but hold it inside where it is never revealed?

Jesus told us that hatred for a brother is equivalent to murder (Matt. 5:22). Thus, sinful anger can occur in the mind, even if it is never translated into overt behavior.[7]

Many psychologists seem to feel that all anger should be ventilated or verbalized. They say it is emotionally and physically harmful to repress or withhold any intense feeling. Can you harmonize this scientific understanding with the scriptural commandment that "every man [should] be swift to hear, slow to speak, slow to wrath: For the wrath of man worketh not the righteousness of God" (Jas. 1:19,20).

Let me state one thing of which I am absolutely certain: *Truth is unity.* In other words, when complete understanding is known about a given topic, then there will be no disagreement between science and the Bible. Therefore, when these two sources of knowledge appear to be in direct contradiction—as in the matter of anger— then there is either something wrong with our interpretation of Scripture or else the scientific premise is false. Under no circumstance, however, will the Bible be found to err. It was inspired by the Creator of the universe, and He does not make mistakes!

In regard to the psychological issues involved in your question, there is undoubtedly some validity to the current view that feelings of anger should not be encapsulated and internalized. When *any* powerful, negative emotion is forced from conscious thought while it is raging full strength, it has the potential of ripping and tearing us from within. The process by which we cram a strong feeling into the unconscious mind is called "repression," and it is psychologically hazardous. The pressure that it generates will usually appear elsewhere in the form of depression, anxiety, tension, or in an entire range of physical disorders.

We must harmonize the psychological finding that anger should be ventilated with the biblical commandment that we be "slow to wrath." Personally, I do not find these objectives to be in contradiction. God does not want us to "repress" our anger—sending it unresolved into the memory bank. Why else did the Apostle Paul tell us to settle our irritations before sundown each day (Eph. 4:26), effectively preventing an accumulation of seething hostility with the passage of time?

But how can intense negative feelings be resolved or ventilated without blasting away at the offender—an act which is specifically prohibited by Scripture? Are there other ways of releasing pent-up emotions? Yes, including those that follow:

By making the irritation a matter of prayer.

By explaining our negative feelings to a mature and understanding "third party" who can advise and lead.

By going to an offender and showing a spirit of love and forgiveness.

By understanding that God often permits the most frustrating and agitating events to occur, so as to teach us patience and help us grow.

By realizing that *no* offense by another person could possibly equal our guilt before God, yet He has forgiven us; are we not obligated to show the same mercy to others?

These are just a few of the mechanisms and attitudes which act to neutralize a spirit of resentment.[8]

I have a very unhappy and miserable neighbor who can't get along with anybody. She has fought with everyone she knows at one time or another. I decided that I was going to make friends with her if it was humanly possible, so I went out of my way to be kind and compassionate. I thought I had made progress toward this goal until she knocked on the front door one day and attacked me verbally. She

had misunderstood something I said to another neighbor, and she came to my house to "tell me off." This woman said all the mean things she could think of, including some very insulting comments about my children, husband, and our home.

I was agitated by her attempt to hurt me when I had tried to treat her kindly, and I reacted with irritation. We stood arguing with each other at the front door and then she left in a huff. I feel bad about the conflict now, but I don't know if I could handle it better today. What should have been my reaction?

Perhaps you realize that you missed the greatest opportunity you will probably ever have to accomplish your original objective of winning her friendship. It is difficult to convince someone of your love and respect during a period of shallow amicability. By contrast, your response to a vicious assault can instantly reveal the Christian values by which you live.

What if you had said for example, "Mary, I don't know what you heard about me, but I think there's been a misunderstanding of what I said. Why don't you come in and we'll talk about it over a cup of coffee."

Everything that you had attempted to accomplish through the previous months might have been achieved on that morning. I admit that it takes great courage and maturity to return kindness for hostility, but we are commanded by Jesus to do just that. He said in Matthew 5:43,44:

> Ye have heard that it hath been said, Thou shalt love thy neighbor, and hate thine enemy. But I say unto you, Love your enemies, bless them that curse you, do good to them that hate you, and pray for them which despitefully use you, and persecute you (KJV).[9]

What do you have to say to the many people who sincerely try to control their anger, but who get irritated and frustrated and still lose their temper time and time again? How can they bring this area under control? Or is it possible?

It has been my observation that the Lord often leads his children, including those with rampaging tempers, in a patient and progressively insistent manner. It begins with a mild sense of condemnation in the area where God wants us to grow and improve. Then as time goes by, a failure to respond is followed by a sense of guilt and awareness of divine disapproval. We are subsequently led to a time of intense awareness of God's requirements. We hear His message revealed (perhaps unwittingly) by the pastor on Sunday morning and in the books we read and even in secular programs on radio and television. It seems as though the whole word is organized to convey the same decree from the Lord. And finally, we come to a crisis point where God says, "You understand what I want. *Now do it!*"

Growth in the Christian life depends on obedience in those times of crisis. The believer who refuses to accept the new obligation despite unmistakable commandments from God is destined to deteriorate spiritually. From that moment forward, he begins to drift away from his Master. But for the Christian who accepts the challenge, regardless of how difficult it may be, his growth and enlightenment are assured.

John Henry Jowett said, "The will of God will never lead you where the grace of God cannot keep you." This means that the Lord won't demand something of you which He doesn't intend to help you implement.[10]

There are times when it is obvious that my kid is *trying* to provoke my

anger, just for the fun of it. Why would he want to upset me when he knows I love him?

It may be the result of a power play between him and you. Indeed, there are times when I think children understand this struggle for control even better than their parents who are bogged down with adult responsibilities and worries. That is why so many kids are able to win the contest of wills; they devote their *primary* effort to the game, while we grown-ups play only when we must. One father overheard his five-year-old daughter, Laura, say to her little sister who was doing something wrong, "Mmmm, I'm going to tell Mommie on you. No! I'll tell Daddy. He's worse!" Laura had evaluated the disciplinary measures of her two parents, and concluded that one was more effective than the other.

This same child was observed by her father to have become especially disobedient and defiant. She was irritating other family members and looking for ways to avoid minding her parents. Her dad decided not to confront her directly about this change in behavior, but to punish her consistently for every offense until she settled down. Thus, for three or four days, he let Laura get away with nothing. She was spanked, stood in the corner, and sent to her bedroom. At the conclusion of the fourth day, she was sitting on the bed with her father and younger sister. Without provocation, Laura pulled the hair of the toddler who was looking at a book. Her dad promptly thumped her on the head with his large hand. Laura did not cry, but sat in silence for a moment or two, and then said, "Hurrummph! All my tricks are not working!"

If the reader will recall his own childhood years, he will probably remember similar events in which the disciplinary techniques of adults were analyzed consciously and their weaknesses probed. When I was a child, I once spent the night with a rambunctious friend who seemed to know every move his parents were going to make. Earl was like a military general who had deciphered the enemy code, permitting him to outmaneuver his opponents at every turn. After we were tucked into our own twin beds that night, he gave me an astounding description of his father's temper.

Earl said, "When my dad gets very angry, he uses some really bad words that will amaze you." (He listed three or four startling examples from past experience.)

I replied, "I don't believe it!"

Mr. Walker was a very tall, reserved man who seemed to have it all together. I just couldn't conceive of his saying the words Earl had quoted.

"Want me to prove it to you?" said Earl mischievously. "All we have to do is keep on laughing and talking instead of going to sleep. My dad will come and tell us to be quiet over and over, and he'll get madder and madder every time he has to settle us down. Then you'll hear his cuss words. Just wait and see."

I was a bit dubious about this plan, but I did want to see the dignified Mr. Walker at his profane best. So Earl and I kept his poor father running back and forth like a Yo-Yo for over an hour. And as predicted, he became more intense and hostile each time he returned to your bedroom. I was getting very nervous and would have called off the demonstration, but Earl had been through it all before. He kept telling me, "It won't be long now."

Finally, about midnight, it happened. Mr. Walker's patience expired. He came thundering down the hall toward our room, shaking the entire house as his feet pounded the floor. He burst through the bedroom door and leaped on Earl's bed, flailing at the boy who was safely buried beneath three or four layers of blankets. Then from his lips came a stream of words that had seldom reached my tender ears. I was shocked, but Earl was delighted.

Even while his father was whacking the covers with his hand and screaming his profanity, Earl raised up and shouted to me, "Did ya hear 'em? Huh? Didn't I tell ya? I told ya he would say it!" It's a wonder that Mr. Walker didn't kill his son at that moment!

I lay awake that night thinking about the episode and made up my mind *never* to let a child manipulate me like that when I grew up. Don't you see how important disciplinary techniques are to a child's respect for his parents? When a forty-five-pound bundle of trouble can deliberately reduce his powerful mother or father to a trembling, snarling mass of frustrations, then something changes in their relationship. Something precious is lost. The child develops an attitude of contempt which is certain to erupt during the stormy adolescent years to come. I sincerely wish every adult understood that simple characteristic of human nature."

SECTION EIGHT
Understanding Guilt

My wife and I are new Christians, and we now realize that we raised our kids by the wrong principles. They're grown now, but we continue to worry about the past, and we feel great regret for our failures as parents. Is there anything we can do at this late date?

Let me deal, first, with the awful guilt you are obviously carrying. There's hardly a parent alive who does not have some regrets and painful memories of their failures as a mother or a father. Children are infinitely complex, and we cannot be perfect parents any more than we can be perfect human beings. The pressures of living are often enormous, and we get tired and irritated; we are influenced by our physical bodies and our emotions, which sometimes prevent us from saying the right things and being the model we should. We don't always handle our children as unemotionally as we wish we had, and it's very common to look back a year or two later and see how wrong we were in the way we approached a problem.

All of us experience these failures! *No one does a job perfectly!* That's why each of us should get alone with the Creator of parents and children, saying,

"Lord, You know my inadequacies. You know my weaknesses, not only in parenting, but in every area of life. I did the best I could, but it wasn't good enough. As You broke the fishes and the loaves to feed the five thousand, now take my meager effort and use it to bless my family. Make up for the things I did wrong. Satisfy the needs that I have not satisfied. Wrap Your great arms around my children, and draw them close to You. And be there when they stand at the great crossroads between right and wrong. All I can give is my best, and I've done that. Therefore, I submit to You my children and myself and the job I did as a parent. The outcome now belongs to You."

I know God will honor that prayer, even for parents whose job is finished. The Lord does not want you to suffer from guilt over events you can no longer influence. The past is the past. Let it die, never to be resurrected. Give the situation to God, and let Him have it. I think you'll be surprised to learn that you're no longer alone![1]

As a psychologist, would you explain what the conscience is and how it works in the mind?

That question (what is the conscience?) was asked among children ages five through nine by the *National Enquirer* a few years ago. One six-year-old said a conscience is the spot inside that "burns if you're not good." A six-year-old boy said he didn't know, but thought it had something to do with feeling bad when you "kicked girls or little dogs." And a nine-year-old explained it as a voice inside that says "No" when you want to do something like beat up your little brother. Her conscience had "saved him a lot of times!"

Adults have also found the conscience difficult to define. Technically speaking, the conscience is a God-given mental faculty that permits us to recognize the difference between right and wrong. And guilt is the uncomfortable feeling that occurs when we violate this inner code of ethics.

In other words, guilt is a message of disapproval from the conscience which says, in effect, "You should be ashamed of yourself!"[2]

If guilt conveys a condemning message from our consciences, is it accurate to say that guilt feelings always contain a message of disapproval from God, too?

No. Let me state with the strongest emphasis that God is *not* the author of all such discomfort. Some feelings of guilt are obviously inspired by the devil, and have nothing to do with the commandments, values, or judgments of our Creator. They can even be a powerful weapon Satan uses against us. By setting an ethical standard which is impossible to maintain, he can generate severe feelings of condemnation and spiritual discouragement.[3]

Would you give some examples of a guilty conscience which God does not inspire? Can a person really feel crushing disapproval and yet be blameless before God?

Categorically, yes! I served for a decade in the Division of Child Development at Children's Hospital of Los Angeles. We saw children throughout the year who were victims of various metabolic problems, most of which caused mental retardation in our young patients. Furthermore, most of these medical problems were produced by genetic errors—that is, each parent contributed a defective gene at the moment of conception which resulted in an unhealthy child being born. When a mother and father realized that they were individually responsible for the distorted, broken, intellectually damaged child before them, the impact was often disastrous. A sense of guilt swept over some parents in such enormous quantities that the family was destroyed by its impact.

Now, it is obvious that God is not the author of this kind of disapproval. He knows—even better than we—that the grief-stricken parents did not intentionally produce a defective child. Their genetic system simply malfunctioned. Certainly our merciful Creator would not hold them responsible for a consequence which they could not have anticipated or avoided. Nevertheless, guilt is often unbearable for parents who hold *themselves* personally responsible for unavoidable circumstances.

Parenthood itself can be a very guilt-producing affair. Even when we give it our best effort, we can see our own failures and mistakes reflected in the lives of our children. We in the Western world are extremely vulnerable to family-related guilt. One mother whom I know walked toward a busy street with her three-year-old daughter. The little toddler ran ahead and stopped on the curb until her mother told her it was safe to cross. The woman was thinking about something else and nodded in approval when the little child asked, "Can I go now, Mommy?"

The youngster ran into the street and was struck full force by a semitrailer truck. The mother gasped in terror as she watched the front and back wheels of the truck crush the life from her precious little girl. The hysterical woman, screaming in anguish and grief, ran to the road and gathered the broken remains of the child in her arms. She had killed her own daughter who depended on her for safety. This mother will *never* escape the guilt of that moment. The "videotape recording" has been rerun a million times in her tormented mind—picturing a trusting baby asking her mother if it was safe to cross the street. Clearly, God has not placed that guilt on the heartbroken woman, but her suffering is no less real.

I could give many other examples of severe guilt which were seemingly self-inflicted or imposed by circumstances. Clearly, at least in my opinion, guilt is not necessarily reflective of God's disapproval.[4]

Would you explain your statement that a sense of guilt is sometimes inspired by Satan?

Second Corinthians 11:14 indicates that Satan presents himself as "an angel of light," meaning he speaks as a false representative of God. Accordingly, it has been my observation that undeserved guilt is one of the most powerful weapons in the devil's arsenal. By seeming to ally himself with the voice of the Holy Spirit, Satan uses the conscience to accuse, torment, and berate his victims. What better tool for spiritual discouragement could there be than feelings of guilt which cannot be "forgiven"—because they do not represent genuine disapproval from God?

The Bible describes Satan as being enormously cunning and vicious. He is not at all like the comical character depicted in popular literature, with a pitchfork and pointed tail. He is a "roaring lion, seeking whom he might devour"; in fact, he is a threat even to those whom God has elected and received as His own. Thus, it has been my observation that Satan does not give up on the committed Christian—he merely attacks from a different direction. One of those directions is undeserved and irrational guilt.[5]

Would you describe more completely the nature of the conscience and how it functions? You implied earlier that a person's sense of guilt is dependent, in part, on what he was taught in childhood. Is that correct?

The subject of the conscience is an extremely complex and weighty topic. Philosophers and theologians have struggled with its meaning for centuries and their views have been characterized by disharmony and controversy from the beginning. Since I am neither a philosopher nor a theologian, I am keenly aware of the deep water in which we tread and have attempted to focus my views on the psychological aspects of the topic.

Concerning influences of childhood instruction on the conscience, the great German philosopher, Immanuel Kant, strongly opposed that concept. He stated unequivocally that the conscience was *not* the product of experience but was an inherited capacity of the soul. I believe most child psychologists today with disagree with Kant on this point. A person's conscience is largely a gift from his parents—from their training and instruction and approval and disapproval. The way right and wrong are taught throughout the first decade of life will never be completely forgotten—even though it may be contradicted later.[6]

That obviously places a tremendous responsibility on us as parents, doesn't it?

The proper "programming" of the conscience is one of the most difficult jobs associated with parenthood, and the one that requires the greatest wisdom. Fifty years ago, parents were more likely to produce excessive guilt in their children. Now, I feel, we have gone much too far in the other direction—in some cases teaching that nothing is sinful or harmful.[7]

You have shown that some guilt does not come from the judgment of the voice of God. In other words, one can feel guilty when he is innocent before

God. Now, how about the opposite side of that coin. Does the absence of guilt mean we are blameless in the sight of the Creator? Can I depend on my conscience to let me know when God is displeased with me?

Apparently, not always. There are many examples of vicious, evil people who seem to feel no guilt for their actions. We can't know for sure, of course, but there is no evidence that Adolf Hitler or Joseph Stalin experienced any serious measure of self-condemnation toward the end of their lives, despite the torment they inflicted on the world.

My point is that the voice of disapproval from within is a fragile thing in some people. It can be seared and ignored until its whisper of protest is heard no longer. Perhaps the most effective silencer for the conscience is found in widespread social opinions. If everybody is doing it—the reasoning goes—it can't be very harmful or sinful.

One study revealed that a very large percent of today's college students now feel it is OK (i.e., not guilt-producing) to have sexual intercourse with someone they have dated and "like a lot." One quarter of all individuals of college age have shared a bedroom with a member of the opposite sex for three months or more. You see, if these same "liberated" young people had participated in that kind of sexual behavior twenty years ago, most of them would have had to deal with feelings of guilt and remorse. Now, however, they are lulled into a false sense of security by the fact that their behavior is "socially acceptable." Individual guilt is partially a product of collective attitudes and concepts of morality, despite the fact that God's standards are eternal and are not open to revision or negotiation. His laws will be in force even if the whole world rejects them, as in the days of Noah.

I am saying that the conscience is an imperfect mental faculty. There are times when it condemns us for mistakes and human frailties that can't be avoided; at other times it will remain silent in the face of indescribable wickedness.[8]

What am I to do with my conscience, then? Is it to be ignored altogether? Does God not speak through this mental faculty?

Let's turn to the Scripture for answers to those questions. Direct reference is made to the conscience in dozens of passages throughout the Word. I have listed a few of those references, as follows, where the Bible refers to a—

"weak conscience" 1 Corinthians 8:7

"defiled conscience" Titus 1:15

"conscience void of offense" Acts 24:16

"pure conscience" 1 Timothy 3:9

"good conscience" Acts 23:1; Hebrews 13:18

"conscience seared with a hot iron" 1 Timothy 4:2

"testimony of our conscience" 2 Corinthians 1:12

the "answer of a good conscience toward God" 1 Peter 3:21

We simply cannot deny the existence of the conscience or the fact that the Holy Spirit influences us through it. Especially pertinent to this point is Romans 9:1, "I am speaking the truth as a Christian, and my own conscience, enlightened by the Holy Spirit, assures me it is no lie" (NEB).

Another Scripture which puts the conscience in proper perspective is found in Romans 2:14, and is quoted as follows:

> When the gentiles, who have no knowledge of the Law, act in accordance with it by the light of nature, they show that they have a law in themselves, for they demonstrate the effect of a law operat-

> ing in their own hearts. Their *own con-*
> *sciences endorse the existence of such a*
> *law, for there is something which con-*
> *demns or excuses their actions* (Phil-
> lips, emphasis added).

There it is in definite terms. The conscience is a reality, and the Holy Spirit
makes use of it. On the other hand, the
conscience has been shown to be unreliable
on occasions. That contradiction poses a
difficult dilemma for us as Christians; we
must learn to separate the true from the
untrue, the real from the imagined, the
right from the wrong. How can we discern,
for sure, the pleasure and displeasure of
our loving God when the voice from within
is somewhat unpredictable?[9]

You are obviously not suggesting that we ignore our consciences altogether, are you?

Most certainly not. As we have seen, the
conscience is often specifically illuminated
by the Holy Spirit and we *must not* disregard His leadings. My words to this point
could offer ammunition for the confirmed
rationalizer who wants to do his own thing
anyway. However, my purpose is not to
weaken the importance of the conscience,

but rather to help us interpret its meaning more effectively.

Guilt is an expression of the conscience which is a product of our emotions. It is a *feeling* of disapproval which is conveyed to the rational mind by what we might call the "Department of the Emotions." Working steadily in the Department of the Emotions is the "Internal Committee on Ethics and Morality"—a group of stern little fellows who review all our actions and attitudes. Nothing that we do escapes their attention, and they can be most offensive when they observe a difference between the way things are and the way they ought to be. However, the condemnation that they issue (and even their approval) is subject to error; they are biased by what they have seen and heard, and they sometimes make mistakes. Therefore, before the judgment of the Committee of Ethics and Morality is accepted as Truth, it must be tested within two other "departments" of the mind. The emotion of condemnation cannot be ignored, but it shouldn't be allowed to stand unchallenged either.

Thus, a *feeling of guilt* must be referred to the "Department of the Intellect" for further evaluation and confirmation.

There it is tested against rational criteria: What does my pastor recommend? What does my own judgment say about the rightness or wrongness of the behavior in question? Is it reasonable that God would hold me responsible for what I've done or thought?

And, of course, the ultimate standard on which guilt is evaluated must be the holy Scripture. What does the Bible say on the matter? If it is not directly mentioned in the Word, what underlying principle is implied? In this way, guilt is evaluated for its validity according to the intellectual process of reason.

There will be times when guilt will originate not in the emotions, but in the intellect itself. Suppose a person is studying the Bible and reads Jesus' words, "All liars will have their place in the lake of fire." He immediately remembers his distorted income tax return, and the numerous "white lies" he has told. The matter is instantaneously referred to the "Department of Emotions" and guilt ensues.

But there is a third division of the mind which must review the decisions of the emotions and the intellect. It is called the "Department of the Will." This is a vitally important mental faculty, for it deals with the person's intent. I personally believe no guilt should be considered to have come from God unless the behavior was an expression of willful disobedience.

Remember Jesus' words as he hung in agony on the cross, while being mocked by the Roman soldiers who put him there. He looked down at them and said, "Father, forgive them." We might ask "Why are they not to blame?" and hear His reply, "they *know not* what they do." Jesus did not hold them accountable for the most evil crime in history, because the perpetrators were ignorant of their wrongdoing.

It is with great comfort that I rest in that same relationship with God. I am certain that there are times when I do the opposite of what He wants. In my humanness—in my partial understanding—I undoubtedly fall short of His best for my life. But I believe that my merciful Father judges me according to the expression of my will. When He has told me what He requires and I refuse to obey, then I stand without excuse before Him.

When we are genuinely culpable before God Almighty, guilt will be validated by all three "departments" of the mind. In some ways, they operate as a system of "checks and balances"—as we intended for the executive, legislative, and judicial branches of the U.S. Government. Each division interacts with the work of the other two and keeps them from gaining unhealthy predominance.[10]

Interpretation of Impressions

Whenever I want to know the will of God in a particular matter, I wait for Him to make me feel positive or negative about it. Do you think that is an effective method of discerning the "mind of God"?

Determining the will of God by means of feelings or impressions always reminds me of the exciting day I completed my formal education at the University of Southern California and was awarded a doctoral degree. My professors shook my hand and offered their congratulations, and I walked from the campus with the prize I had sought so diligently. On the way home in the car that day, I expressed my appreciation to God for His obvious blessing on my life, and I asked Him to use me in any way he chose. The presence of the Lord seemed very near as I communed with Him in that little red Volkswagen.

Then, as I turned a corner (I remember the precise spot), I was seized by a strong impression which conveyed this unmistakable message: "You are going to lose someone very close to you within the next twelve months. A member of your immediate family will die, but when it happens, don't be dismayed. Just continue trusting and depending on me."

Since I had not been thinking about death or anything that would have explained the sudden appearance of this premonition, I was alarmed by the threatening thought. My heart thumped a little harder as I contemplated who might die and in what manner the end would come. Nevertheless, when I reached my home that night, I told no one about the experience.

One month passed without tragedy or human loss. Two and three months sped by, and still the hand of death failed to visit my family. Finally, the anniversary of my morbid impression came and went without consequence. It has now been more than a decade since that frightening day in the Volkswagen, and there have been no catastrophic events in either my family or among my wife's closest relatives. The impression has proved invalid.

Through my subsequent counseling experience and professional responsibilities, I have learned that my phony impression was not unique. Similar experiences are common, particularly among those who have not adjusted well to the challenge of living.

For example, a thirty-year-old wife and mother came to me for treatment of persistent anxiety and depression. In relating her history she described an episode that occurred in a church service when she was sixteen years old. Toward the end of the sermon, she "heard" this alarming message from God: "Jeanie, I want you to die so that others will come to Me."

Jeanie was absolutely terrified. She felt as though she stood on the gallows with the hangman's noose dangling above her head. In her panic, she jumped from her seat and fled through the doors of the building, sobbing as she ran. Jeanie felt she would commit a sin if she revealed her impression to anyone, so she kept it to herself. For fourteen years she has awaited the execution of this divine sentence, still wondering when the final moment will arrive. Nevertheless, she appears to be in excellent health today, fourteen years later.

From these example and dozens more, I have come to regard the interpretation of impressions as risky business, at best.[1]

Are you saying that God does not speak directly to the heart—that all impressions are false and unreliable?

Certainly not. It is the expressed purpose of the Holy Spirit to deal with human beings in a most personal and intimate way, convicting, directing and influencing. However, some people seem to find it very difficult to distinguish the voice of God from other sounds within.[2]

Do some of those "other sounds" represent the influence of Satan?

Yes. That is why he is described in profoundly evil terms in the Bible, leaving little room for doubt as to his motives or nature. His character is presented as wicked, malignant, subtle, deceitful, fierce, and cruel. He is depicted as a wolf, roaring lion, and a serpent. Among the titles ascribed to Satan are these: "Murderer," "Dragon," "Old Serpent," "Wicked One," "Liar," "Prince of the Devils," and more than twenty other names which describe a malicious and incomparably evil nature.

These scriptural descriptions of Satan are written for a purpose: we should recognize that the "Father of Lies" has earned his reputation at the expense of those he has damned! And there is no doubt in my mind that he often uses destructive impressions to implement his evil purposes.[3]

You said your premonition of impending death occurred while you were praying. Is it really possible for Satan to speak in the midst of an earnest prayer?

Was not Jesus tempted by Satan while He was on a forty-day prayer and fasting journey in the wilderness?

Yes, the devil can speak at any time. Let me go a step further: harmful impressions can bear other earmarks of divine revelation. They can occur and recur for months at a time. They can be as intense as any other emotion in life. They can be verified by Christian friends and can even seemingly be validated by striking passages of Scripture.[4]

Are some impressions and feelings of our own making?

In a way, they all are. By that I mean

that all of our impulses and thoughts are vulnerable to our physical condition and psychological situation at any given moment. Haven't you noticed that your impressions are affected by the amount of sleep you had last night, the state of your health, your level of confidence at that time, and dozens of other forces which impinge upon your decision-making processes? We are trapped in these "earthen vessels," and our perception is necessarily influenced by our humanness.[5]

I have sometimes wondered if my impressions don't obediently tell me what I most want to hear. For example, I felt greatly led to take a new job that offered a higher salary and shorter working hours.

That reminds me of the minister who received a call to a much larger and stronger church than he ever expected to lead. He replied, "I'll pray about it while my wife packs."

It is very difficult to separate the "want to" from our interpretation of God's will. The human mind will often obediently convince itself of anything in order to have its own way. Perhaps the most striking example of this self-delusion occurred with a young couple I later counseled, who had decided to engage in sexual intercourse before marriage. Since the young man and woman were both reared in the church, they had to find a way to lessen the guilt from this forbidden act. So, they actually got down on their knees and prayed about what they were going to do, and received "assurance" that it was all right to continue![6]

I heard a man say that he dreamed he should marry a certain woman. Does God ever speak to us in that way through dreams today?

I don't know. He certainly used this method of communicating in Old Testament times; however, it appears to me that the use of dreams has been less common since the advent of the Holy Spirit, because the Spirit was sent to be our source of enlightenment. (See John 16.)

Even in prior times, Jeremiah called dreams "chaff" when compared to the Word of God. Personally, I would not accept a dream as being authentic, regardless of how vivid it seemed, until the same content was verified in other ways.[7]

What do you mean by having the "content verified in other ways"?

I mean that the "direction" given to me in a dream should be supported by other pieces of information that I would receive. For example, suppose I dream that I am called to Africa as a medical missionary. Before I start packing, I should consider some other factors: Am I qualified by training, experience, interests? Have there been any direct invitations or opportunities presented?

John Wesley wrote in the nineteenth century, "Do not hastily ascribe things to God. Do not easily suppose dreams, voices, impressions, visions, or revelations to be from God. They may be from Him. They may be nature. They may be from the Devil. Therefore, believe not every spirit, but 'try the spirits whether they be from God.'"[8]

What is the purpose of dreams, from a scientific and psychological point of view?

Dreams appear to have two basic purposes: they reflect wish fulfillment, giving expression to the things we long for; and second, they ventilate anxiety and the stresses we experience during waking hours. They also serve to keep us asleep when we are drifting toward consciousness. Dreams are being studied at length in experimental laboratories today, although their nature is still rather poorly understood.[9]

If what we feel is so unreliable and dangerous, then how can we even know the will of God? How can we tell the difference between the leadings of the Holy Spirit and subtle, evil influences of Satan himself?

Let's look to the Scripture for a word of encouragement:

Concerning Christ's power to help in time of temptation: "Because he himself suffered when he was tempted, he is able to help those who are being tempted" (Heb. 2:18 NIV).

Concerning the power of God to convey his will to us: "And this is my prayer. That the God of our Lord Jesus Christ, the all-glorious Father, will give you spiritual wisdom and the insight to know more of him: that you may receive that inner illumination of the spirit which will make you realize how great is the hope to which he is calling you—the magnificence and splendour of the inheritance promised to Christians—and how tremendous is the power available to us who believe in God" (Eph. 1:16-19 Phillips).

Concerning the power of God over Satan: "You, my children, who belong to God have already defeated them, because the one who lives in you is stronger than the anti-Christ in the world" (1 John 4:4 Phillips).

Concerning the divine promise to lead and guide us: "I will instruct thee and teach thee in the way which thou shalt go: I will guide thee with mine eye" (Psa. 32:8 KJV).

In paraphrased form, these four Scriptures offer these promises:

1. Jesus was tempted by Satan when He was on earth, so He is fully equipped to deal with him now on our behalf.

2. "Inner illumination" and "spiritual wisdom" are made available to us by the God who controls the entire universe.

3. Satan's influence is checkmated by the omniscient power of God, living within us.

4. Like a father leading his trusting child, our Lord will guide our steps and teach us His wisdom.

These four Scriptures are supported by dozens more which promise God's guidance, care, and leadership in our lives.[10]

Then how do you account for the experiences of those Christians who grope with uncertainty in the darkness and

eventually stumble and fall? How do you explain incidents whereby Satan traps them into believing and acting on his lies?

The Scripture, again, provides its own answer to that troubling question. We are told in 1 John 4:1: "Don't trust every spirit, dear friends of mine, but test them to discover whether they come from God or not" (Phillips). A similar commandment is given in 1 Thessalonians 5:21: "Prove all things; hold fast that which is good" (KJV). In other words, it is our responsibility to "test" and "prove" all things—including the validity of our impressions. To do otherwise is to give Satan an opportunity to defeat us, despite the great power of the Holy Spirit who lives within. We would not have been told to test the spirits if there were no danger in them.[11]

By what means can I "test" my own feelings and impressions? What are the steps necessary to "prove" the will of God?

The best answer I've read for those questions was written in 1892 by Martin Wells Knapp. In his timeless little booklet entitled *Impressions,* he described those impulses and leadings that come from above (from God) versus those that originate from below (from Satan). Just as the Holy Spirit may tell us by impressions what His will is concerning us, so also can our spiritual enemies tell us by impressions what their will is. And unfortunately, there is often a striking resemblance between the two kinds of messages. According to Knapp, one of the objectives of Satan is to get the Christian to lean totally on his impressions, accepting them uncritically as the absolute voice of God. When this occurs, "the devil has got all he wants."

When seeking God's will, Knapp recommends that each impression be evaluated very carefully to see if it reflects four distinguishing features:

Scriptural. Is the impression in harmony with the Bible? Guidance from the Lord is *always* in accordance with the Holy Scripture, and this gives us an infallible point of reference and comparison.

The most important aspect of this first test is that *the entire Bible be used* instead of the selection of "proof texts" or "chance texts." A reader can find support for almost any viewpoint if he lifts individual verses or partial phrases out of context.

Right. Knapps second test of impressions involves the matter of rightness. "Impressions which are from God are always right," says Knapp. "They may be contrary to our feelings, our prejudices and our natural inclinations, but they are always right. They will stand all tests."[12]

I am acquainted with a family which was destroyed by an impression that could not have passed the test: Is it right? Although there were four little children in the home, the mother felt she was "called" to leave them and enter full-time evangelistic work. On a very short notice, she abandoned the children who needed her so badly, and left them in the care of their father who worked six and seven days a week.

The consequence was devastating. The youngest in the family lay awake at night, crying for his mommy. The older children had to assume adult responsibilities which they were ill prepared to carry. There was no one at home to train and love and guide the development of the lonely little family. I simply cannot believe the mother's impression was from God because it was neither scriptural nor "right" to leave the children. I suspect that she had other motives for fleeing her home, and Satan provided her with a seemingly noble explanation to cover her tracks.

As Knapp said, "Millions of impressions, if compelled to answer the simple question, 'Are you right?' will blush and hesitate and squirm, and finally in confusion, retire."

Providential. In explaining the importance of providential circumstances, Knapp quoted Hannah Whitall Smith, writing in *The Christian's Secret of a Happy Life:*

> If a leading is from the Holy Spirit, "the way will always open for it." The Lord assures us of this when he says: "When he putteth forth his own sheep, he goeth before them, and the sheep follow him: for they know his voice" (John 10:4, KJV). Notice here the expression "goeth before" and "follow." He goes before to open the way, and we are to follow in the way thus opened. It is never a sign of divine leading when a Christian insists on opening his own way, and riding roughshod over all opposing things. If the Lord goes before us He will open all doors before us, and we shall not need ourselves to hammer them down.

Reasonable. The Apostle Paul referred to the Christian life as a "reasonable service."

Accordingly, the will of God can be expected to be in harmony with "spiritually enlightened judgment. We will not be asked to do absurd and ridiculous things which are devoid of judgment and common sense. Knapp said, "God has given us reasoning powers for a purpose, and he respects them, appeals to them, and all of his leadings are in unison with them."[13]

Of Knapp's four criteria, "providential circumstances" seems hardest to apply. Can you give an example?

Personally, I have come to depend heavily on providential circumstances to speak to me of God's will. My impressions serve as little more than "hunches" which cause me to pay closer attention to more concrete evidence around me. For example, in 1970 my wife and I considered the wisdom of selling our house and buying one better suited to the needs of our growing family. However, there were many factors to consider in such a move. The lifestyle, values, and even the safety of a family is influenced by the neighborhood in which it resides. I felt it would be foolish to sell our home and buy a new one without seeking the guidance of the Lord.

After making the possibility a matter of

prayer, I felt I should offer our house for sale without listing it with a realtor. If it sold I would know that God had revealed His leading through this providential circumstance. For two weeks a For Sale sign stood unnoticed in the front yard. It didn't attract a single call or knock on the door, and my prayer was answered in the negative.

I took down the sign and waited twelve months before asking the same question of the Lord. This time, the house sold for my asking price without a nickel being spent on advertising or real estate fees. There was no doubt in my mind that the Lord had another home in mind for us.[14]

How do you know that the sale of your house was not explained by economic circumstances or simply by the fact that an interested buyer came along? Can you say, definitely, that God determined the outcome?

Matters of faith can never be proved; they always have to be "the substance of things hoped for, the evidence of things not seen" (Heb. 11:1, KJV). It would be impossible to make a skeptic acknowledge that God influenced the sale of our house, just as the same unbeliever would doubt my conversion experience wherein I became a Christian. You see, it was not the unadvertised sale of my house that convinced me that God was involved in the issue—it was that I met with Him on my knees in prayer and asked for His specific guidance and direction. I have reason to believe that He cares about me and my family, and hears me when I ask for His leadership. Therefore, my interpretation of the event is based not on facts but on faith. Spiritual experiences must *always* rest on that foundation.[15]

Will there be times when the application of Knapp's four tests still leaves a Christian in a state of doubt about the leadings of the Lord? Or does a committed Christian always know precisely what God wants of him?

Your question is one which is rarely confronted in books dealing with the will of God, but I feel we must meet it head-on. I believe there are times in the lives of most believers when confusion and perplexity are rampant. What could Job have felt, for example, when his world began to crack and splinter? His family members became sick and died, his livestock was wiped out, and he was besieged by boils from the top of his head to the bottom of his feet. But most troubling of all was his inability to make spiritual sense of the circumstances. He knew he hadn't sinned, despite the accusations of his "friends," yet, God must have seemed a million miles away. He said at one point, "Oh, that I knew where to find God—that I could go to his throne and talk with him there" (Job 23:3 TLB). "But I search in vain. I seek him here, I seek him there, and cannot find him. I seek him in his workshop in the North, but cannot find him there; nor can I find him in the South; there, too, he hides himself" (Job 23:8,9 TLB).

Was this experience unique to Job? I don't think so. In my counseling responsibilities with Christian families, I've learned that sincere, dedicated believers go through tunnels and storms, too. We inflict a tremendous disservice on young Christians by making them think only sinners experience confusion and depressing times in their lives.

We must remember that God is not a subservient genie who comes out of a bottle to sweep away each trial and hurdle which blocks our path. Accordingly, He has not promised to lay out an eight-year master plan that delineates every conceivable alternative in the roadway. Rather, He offers us His will for *today* only. Our tomorrows must be met one day at a time, negotiated with a generous portion of faith.[16]

Are you saying there will be times in a Christian's life when God's will and actions may not make sense to him?

Yes, and I regret the shallow teaching today which denies this fact. We are told in the Book of Isaiah, "For my thoughts are not your thoughts, neither are your ways my ways, saith the Lord" (55:8 KJV). Furthermore, the Apostle Paul verified that we "see through a glass darkly." In practical terms, this means that there will be times when God's behavior will be incomprehensible and confusing to us.[17]

Are we to conclude, then, that there are occasions when we will pray for the will of God to be known, and yet we may "hear" no immediate reply?

I think so, but I'm also convinced that God is as close to us and as involved in our situation during those times when we feel nothing, as He is when we are spiritually exhilarated. We are not left to flounder. Rather, our faith is strengthened by these testing periods. The only comforting attitude to hold during these stressful times is beautifully summarized in 2 Corinthians 4:8-10:

> We are pressed on every side by troubles, but not crushed and broken. We are perplexed because we don't know why things happen as they do, but we don't give up and quit. We are hunted down, but God never abandons us. We get knocked down, but we get up again and keep going. These bodies of ours are constantly facing death just as Jesus did; so it is clear to all that it is only the living Christ within [who keeps us safe] (TLB).[18]

I know many people who make their financial decisions on the basis of astrology. Even their business dealings are influenced by their horoscopes. Will you comment on the practice of astrology and whether there are any scientific facts to support it?

Of all the social developments occurring in recent years, none reveals our spiritual poverty more than the current devotion to astrology. I have been amazed by television personalities, politicians, and millions of American young people. Even France's former president, Georges Pompidou, admitted in a press conference that he consulted his astrologer before making important speeches or state decisions.

How ridiculous to think that Adolf Hitler, Queen Elizabeth, Harry Truman, William Shakespeare, Bing Crosby, Willy Mays, Ho Chi Minh, Golda Meir, and I should have everything in common because all of us were born under the sign of Taurus! How stupid to suppose that the success of our business ventures, our health, and even our sex lives are predetermined by the position of the stars and planets on the day of our births! Yet, there are more than 10,000 astrologers currently working in the United States, offering advice on everything from business deals to the compatibility of a man and his dog.

There is not a scrap of scientific evidence to support the validity of such illogical and atheistic notions. In fact, it was an all-knowing astrologist who advised Hitler to attack Russia—his biggest mistake! Nevertheless, millions of believers consult their horoscopes to obtain daily truth and wisdom.

I was recently introduced to a famous Hollywood actor while we sat waiting to appear on a television talk program. My wife was with me to observe the interview, and the actor commented on her attractiveness. He said, "I'll bet you are a Sagittarius, because most pretty girls are born under that sign." I was so appalled by the silliness of his statement that I felt obliged to challenge what he said. Trying not to insult his intelligence (which was difficult), I asked him if he had made any effort to prove his hypothesis. I pointed out how simple it would be, for example, to check the birth date of every girl entered in next year's Miss America or Miss Universe contest. I soon learned that the best way to end a conversation with an astrologist is to begin talking about scientific evidence.

In 1960, the world's astrologers announced that the worst combination of planetary influences in 25,000 years would occur that year. Seven of the nine planets were to appear in a line, which meant bad news for Mother Earth! Indian soothsayers were going crazy in sheer fright, and American skygazers were predicting everything from the drowning of California to the cataclysmic end of the world. But the fateful day came and went, of course, with no more disasters than on any other day. The astrologers had overlooked one fundamental fact: Man's destiny is not controlled by the planets. Both man and the heavenly bodies are under the indisputable authority of Almighty God!

When astrological advice is broadcast on radio or television stations, the announcers often repeat a disclaimer, saying they are not attempting to foster a serious belief in astrology and are providing the horoscopes for fun and entertainment. How about it, then? Is astrology just an amusing pastime for our enjoyment? What about those millions of Americans who depend on the stars to provide direction and meaning each day? Isn't it better that they believe in this myth than to believe in nothing at all? Should we foster a tolerant attitude toward astrology, or should it be seen as an insidious philosophy to be opposed wherever possible?

A widely quoted psychiatrist recently professed that he urges his patients to depend on their astrologers, even though he admits that their predictions are scientifically worthless. I couldn't disagree more totally! Astrology is not only mythical nonsense, but it is dangerous to those who accept its tenets. One serious concern is that it offers a substitute for rational judgment and wisdom. A young man or woman, for example, may choose a marital partner on the basis of compatibility of their charts, without proper regard for the lifetime implications of their decision. Others postpone or disregard needed action because of the "do nothing" advice printed in their horoscopes. There is no way to estimate how many important decisions are based on the stars each day, undoubtedly having a profound impact on family, business, and even governmental affairs. How risky it is to determine one's destiny by the flip of a fickle coin! The naive believer exchanges his understanding of the facts, his common sense, his experience, and his better judgment for a "know it all—tell all" pulp magazine of forecasts. He reminds me of a man confidently leaning against the wind while standing on top of a ten-story building. His body is seemingly held in check as he teeters precariously over the edge of the structure. But sooner or later, the gusts will slacken and the man will suddenly plunge downward in panic. Likewise, the astrology convert is leaning against an apparition which cannot possibly hold him securely in place. Sooner or later, when troubling and fearful circumstances beset him (as will come to everyone), he will reach frantically for something stable and firm to grasp. But he will find little support in the myth and superstition on which he has been leaning. Please believe me when I say I am personally and professionally acquainted with individuals who have taken that frightening plunge. Some fun! Some entertainment![19]

Why do you suppose so many highly educated and intelligent people are willing to follow their horoscopes, when astrology is so baseless and unsupportable?

There are, I feel, three answers to that question:

1. In recent years, a tremendous spiritual vacuum has occurred in the lives of many people who previously believed in God. Now that their God is dead, they are desperate for a substitute who can offer some measure of meaning and purpose to life.

Accordingly, someone has said, "Superstition is the worm that exudes from the grave of a dead faith." In other words, human beings *must* have something in which to believe, and in the absence of a meaningful faith in God, reliance is placed in superstitious nonsense.

2. Astrology is the only "religion" which

imposes no obligation on its followers. One does not have to go to church for it, pay tithes to it, obey it, sing praises to it, be moral and honest for it, or sacrifice for it. And certainly, its followers need not carry a cross nor die in its cause.

All one must do is read and believe the words of its self-appointed priests in the daily newspaper. (Or perhaps pay $3.75 for a supersignificant, individualized horoscope, autographed personally by an IBM computer!)

3. It would be unwise to underestimate the real force behind the current astrological interest; it is clearly the tool of Satan himself. Whenever astrologists do predict events accurately, it is because of the demonic insights of God's greatest adversary.

This is not merely my opinion on the subject, which isn't very important. It is clearly the viewpoint of God Himself, as expressed repeatedly in His Holy Word. The following two quotations from *The Living Bible* serve to summarize his commandments to us regarding the practice of astrology and sorcery:

> Hear the word of the Lord, O Israel: Don't act like the people who make horoscopes and try to read their fate

and future in the stars! Don't be
frightened by predictions such as
theirs, for it is all a pack of lies (Jer.
10:1-3 TLB).

Call out the demon hordes you've wor-
shiped all these years. Call on them to help
you strike deep terror into many hearts
again. You have advisors by the ton—your
astrologers and stargazers, who try to tell
you what the future holds. But they are as
useless as dried grass burning in the fire.
They cannot even deliver themselves!
You'll get no help from them at all. Theirs
is no fire to sit beside to make you warm!
And all your friends of childhood days shall
slip away and disappear, unable to help
(Isa. 47:12-15 TLB).[20]

FINAL COMMENT

My purpose in preparing this book has been to provide practical, "how to" advice regarding everyday problems. Moreover, I wanted to arrange the items in a format that would be easily accessible to those with specific needs or concerns. Having completed that assignment in the form of questions and answers, I would like to conclude by explaining why such a book was thought to be needed, and finally, what philosophy underlies the recommendations expressed.

In previous centuries, adults dealt with personal problems, self-doubt, moods, and depression by themselves, without the aid of professional advice. Since the advent of psychology, however, people have rushed to the "experts" for help, turning to psychiatrists, psychologists, educators, and self-help experts for answers to their questions about the complexities of life.

It is now appropriate that we ask, "What has been the effect of this professional influence?" One would expect that mental health of Americans would exceed that of individuals raised in nations not having this technical assistance. Such has not been the case. Drug abuse, alcoholism, abortion, mental illness, and suicide are rampant and continue their steady rise. In many ways, we have made a mess of life! Of course, I would not be so naive as to blame all these woes on the bad advice of the "experts," but I believe they had played a role in creating the problem. Why? *Because in general, behavioral scientists have lacked confidence in the Judeo-Christian ethic and have disregarded the wisdom of this priceless tradition!*

It appears to me that the twentieth century has spawned a generation of professionals who felt qualified to ignore the commonsense practices of more than 2,000 years, substituting instead their own wobbly-legged insights of the moment. Each authority, writing from his own limited experience and reflecting his own unique biases, has sold us his guesses and suppositions as though they represented Truth itself. One anthropologist, for example, wrote an incredibly gallish article in *The Saturday Evening Post,* November 1968, entitled, "We Scientists Have a Right to Play God." Dr. Edmund Leach stated,

There can be no source for these moral judgments except the scientist himself. In traditional religion, morality was held to derive from God, but God was only credited with the authority to establish and enforce moral rules because He was also credited with supernatural powers of creation and destruction. Those powers have now been usurped by man, and he must take on the moral responsibility that goes with them.

That paragraph summarizes the many ills of our day. Arrogant men like Edmund Leach have argued God out of existence and put themselves in His exalted place. Armed with that authority, they have issued their ridiculous opinions to the public with unflinching confidence. In turn, desperate families grabbed their porous recommendations like life preservers, which often sank to the bottom, taking their passengers down with them.

These false teachings have included the notions that loving discipline is damaging, irresponsibility is healthy, religious instruction is hazardous, defiance is a valuable ventilator of anger, all authority is dangerous, and so on and on it goes. In more recent years, this humanistic perspective has become even more extreme and anti-Christian. For example, one mother told me recently that she works in a youth project which has obtained the consultative services of a certain psychologist. He has been teaching the parents of kids in the program that in order for young girls to grow up with more healthy attitudes toward sexuality, their fathers should have intercourse with them when they are twelve years of age. If you gasped at that suggestion, be assured that it shocked me also. Yet this is where moral relativism leads—this is the ultimate product of a human endeavor which accepts no standards, honors no cultural values, acknowledges no absolutes, and serves no "god" except the human mind. King Solomon wrote about such foolish efforts in Proverbs 14:12: "There is a way which *seemeth* right unto a man, but the end thereof are the ways of death" (KJV, emphasis added).

Now, admittedly, the answers to questions provided in this book also contain many suggestions and perspectives which I have not attempted to validate or prove. How do these writings differ from the unsupported recommendations of those whom I have criticized? The distinction lies in the *source* of the views being presented. The underlying principles expressed herein are not my own innovative insights which would be forgotten in a brief season or two. Instead, they originated with the inspired biblical writers who gave us the foundation for all of life. As such, these principles have been handed down generation after generation to this very day. Our ancestors taught them to their children who taught them to their children, keeping the knowledge alive for posterity. Now, unfortunately, that understanding is being vigorously challenged in some circles and altogether forgotten in others.

Therefore, my purpose in preparing this book has been to verbalize the Judeo-Christian tradition and philosophy regarding family living in its many manifestations. And what is that philosophical foundation? It involves parental control of young children with love and care, a reasonable introduction to self-discipline and responsibility, parental *leadership* which seeks the best interest of the child, respect for the dignity and worth of every member of the family, sexual fidelity between husbands and wives, conformity with the moral laws of God, and it attempts to maximize the physical and mental potential of each individual from infancy forward. That is our game plan.

If the objectives cited above could be boiled at extreme temperatures until only the essential ingredients remained, these four irreducible values would survive unscathed:

1. A belief in the unestimable worth and significance of human life in all dimensions, including the unborn, the aged, the widowed, the mentally retarded, the unattractive, the physically handicapped, and every other condition in which humanness is expressed from conception to the grave.

2. An unyielding dedication to the institution of marriage as a permanent, life-long relationship, regardless of trials, sickness, financial reverses or emotional stresses that may ensue.

3. A dedication to the task of bearing and raising children, even in a topsy-turvy world that denigrates this procreative privilege.

4. A commitment to the ultimate purpose in living: the attainment of eternal life through Jesus Christ our Lord, beginning within our own families and then reaching out to a suffering humanity that does not

know of His love and sacrifice. Compared to this overriding objective, no other human endeavor is of any significance or meaning whatsoever.

The four corners of this Christian perspective have been under severe assault in recent years, yet the philosophy will remain viable for as long as mothers and fathers and children cohabit the face of the earth. It will certainly outlive humanism and the puny efforts of mankind to find an alternative.

NOTES

Key for book abbreviations

DD—*Dare to Discipline,* Tyndale House Publishers, Wheaton, IL, 1970, trade paper.

EM—*Emotions: Can You Trust Them?* Regal Books, Ventura, CA, 1980.

HS—*Hide or Seek: Self-Esteem for the Child*, Fleming H. Revell Company, Old Tappan, NJ, 1979.

PA—*Preparing for Adolescence,* Vision House Publishers, Santa Ana, CA, 1978.

STTM—*Straight Talk to Men and Their Wives,* Word Books, Waco, TX, 1980.

SWC—*The Strong-Willed Child,* Tyndale House Publishers, Wheaton, IL, 1978.

WWW—*What Wives Wish Their Husbands Knew about Women,* Tyndale House Publishers, Wheaton, IL, 1975.

FF—*Focus on the Family* cassette tapes.

Section 1
The Source of Self-Esteem in Children
1. HS 20
2. HS 23-25
3. WWW 36, 37
4. HS 34, 40
5. HS 25, 26
6. HS 31, 32
7. HS 40, 41
8. HS 77, 78
9. HS 45-47
10. HS 48, 49
11. HS 13, 60, 61
12. HS 59, 60
13. WWW 60
14. HS 169, 170

Section 2
Developing Self-Esteem in Children
1. HS 80, 81
2. HS 163-165
3. HS 83
4. HS 83, 84
5. HS 89-91
6. SWC 87, 88
7. HS 97
8. *Ibid.*
9. HS 85
10. HS 85, 86
11. HS 86
12. HS 92, 93
13. HS 86-88
14. HS 68, 69
15. HS 75
16. HS 182, 183
17. HS 71, 72
18. HS 70
19. HS 78, 79
20. *Your Child from 2 to 5,* Morton Edwards, ed., 182-184
21. SWC 88-92

22. HS 176-179

Section 3
Parental Overprotection
1. DD 47, 48
2. HS 107
3. HS 105, 106, 109
4. Domeena C. Renshaw, M.D., *The Hyperactive Child* (Chicago: Nelson-Hall Publishers, 1974), 118-120
5. SWC 216, 217
6. HS 108
7. HS 108, 109
8. SWC 219-222

Section 4
Self-Esteem in Adulthood
1. HS 20, 21
2. WWW 25-28
3. HS 149
4. HS 52
5. WWW 128, 129
6. WWW 37, 40
7. HS 104, 105
8. WWW 22, 23
9. WWW 37-39
10. WWW 40, 41
11. HS 145, 146
12. HS 147, 148
13. HS 146, 147
14. HS 184-187

Section 5
Depression in Women
1. WWW 15
2. WWW 22
3. WWW 41
4. WWW 18, 19
5. HS 70, 73 DD 219-221
6. WWW 51-54
7. EM 118, 119
8. HS 148]
9. STTM 188, 189

Section 6
Understanding Premenstrual Tension
1. *Premenstrual Tension* (cassette)
2. STTM 163
3. WWW 151, 152
4. *Psychology Today* (Santa Cruz, CA: Davis Publishing Co.), February 1972. Used by permission.
5. STTM 164
6. WWW 152
7. STTM 164, 165 WWW 153 *Premenstrual Tension* (cassette)

8. *Premenstrual Tension* (cassette)
9. *Ibid.*
10. WWW 155
11. WWW 155, 156
12. WWW 155

Section 7
A Christian Perspective on Anger
1. EM 9-11
2. EM 85
3. EM 85, 86
4. EM 87, 88
5. EM 91
6. EM 92
7. *Ibid.*
8. EM 92-95
9. EM 101, 102
10. EM 103, 104
11. SWC 108-111

Section 8
Understanding Guilt
1. STTM 76, 77
2. EM 18
3. EM 21
4. EM 21, 22
5. EM 22-24
6. EM 33, 34
7. EM 34
8. EM 24-26
9. EM 26, 27
10. EM 27-30

Section 9
Interpretation of Impressions
1. EM 113-115

2. EM 115
3. EM 115, 116
4. EM 116
5. EM 117, 118
6. EM 118
7. EM 119
8. EM 119, 120
9. EM 120
10. EM 120, 121
11. EM 121, 122
12. This and following quotes are from *Impressions,* Martin Wells Knapp (Revivalist Publishing, 1892).
13. EM 122-125
14. EM 125, 126
15. EM 126, 127
16. EM 128, 129
17. EM 130
18. EM 131
19. WWW 108-111
20. WWW 111, 112

QUESTION INDEX

conscience to let me know when God is displeased
with me? *178*

98. What am I to do with my conscience, then? Is it to be
ignored altogether? Does God not speak through
this mental faculty? *179*

99. You are obviously not suggesting that we ignore our
consciences altogether, are you? *181*

Section 9 Interpretation of Impressions

100. Do you think an effective method of discerning the
"mind of God" is to wait for Him to make me feel
positive or negative about a particular matter? *187*

101. Are you saying that God does not speak directly to
the heart—that all impressions are false and unreliable? *190*

102. Do some of those "other sounds" represent the influence of Satan? *190*

103. Is it really possible for Satan to speak in the midst
of an earnest prayer? *191*

104. Are some impressions and feelings of our own making? *191*

105. I have wondered if my impressions don't obediently
tell me what I most want to hear. *192*

106. I heard a man say that he dreamed he should marry
a certain woman. Does God ever speak to us in that
way through dreams today? *193*

107. What do you mean by having the "content verified in
other ways"? *193, 194*

108. What is the purpose of dreams, from a scientific and
psychological point of view? *194*

109. How can we tell the difference between the leadings
of the Holy Spirit and the subtle, evil influences of
Satan himself? *195*

110. Then how do you account for Christians who grope
blindly or fall into Satan's traps and believe his lies?
196

111. By what means can I "test" my own feelings and impressions and "prove" the will of God? *197*

112. Of Knapp's four criteria, "providential circumstances" seems hardest to apply. Can you give an example? *201*

113. How can you say definitely that God, rather than circumstances, determined the outcome of the sale of
your house? *202*

GENERAL INDEX

Other Living Books Best-Sellers

74 MORE FUN AND CHALLENGING BIBLE CROSSWORDS. This brand-new batch of crosswords features both theme puzzles and general crosswords on a variety of levels, all relating to Bible facts, characters, and terms. 07-0488-6

400 CREATIVE WAYS TO SAY I LOVE YOU by Alice Chapin. Perhaps the flame of love has almost died in your marriage, or you have a good marriage that just needs a little spark. Here is a book of creative, practical ideas for the woman who wants to show the man in her life that she cares. 07-0919-5

ANSWERS by Josh McDowell and Don Stewart. In a question-and-answer format, the authors tackle sixty-five of the most-asked questions about the Bible, God, Jesus Christ, miracles, other religions, and creation. 07-0021-X

ANSWERS TO YOUR FAMILY'S FINANCIAL QUESTIONS by Larry Burkett. Questions about credit, saving, taxes, insurance, and more are answered in this handbook that shows how the Bible can guide our financial lives. 07 0025-2

THE BEST OF BIBLE TRIVIA I: KINGS, CRIMINALS, SAINTS, AND SINNERS by J. Stephen Lang. A fascinating book containing over 1,500 questions and answers about the Bible arranged topically in over 50 categories. Taken from the best-selling **Complete Book of Bible Trivia.** 07-0464-9

THE CHILD WITHIN by Mari Hanes. The author shares insights she gained from God's Word during her own pregnancy. She identifies areas of stress, offers concrete data about the birth process, and points to God's sure promises that he will gently lead those that are with young. 07-0219-0

CHRISTIANITY: THE FAITH THAT MAKES SENSE by Dennis McCallum. New and inquiring Christians will find spiritual support in this readable apologetic, which presents a clear, rational defense for Christianity to those unfamiliar with the Bible. 07-0525-4

COME BEFORE WINTER AND SHARE MY HOPE by Charles R. Swindoll. A collection of brief vignettes offering hope and the assurance that adversity and despair are temporary setbacks we can overcome! 07-0477-0

Other Living Books Best-Sellers

LIFE IS TREMENDOUS! by Charlie "Tremendous" Jones. Believing that enthusiasm makes the difference, Jones shows how anyone can be happy, involved, relevant, productive, healthy, and secure in the midst of a high-pressure, commercialized society. 07-2184-5

LORD, COULD YOU HURRY A LITTLE? by Ruth Harms Calkin. These prayer-poems from the heart of a godly woman trace the inner workings of the heart, following the rhythms of the day and seasons of the year with expectation and love. 07-3816-0

LORD, I KEEP RUNNING BACK TO YOU by Ruth Harms Calkin. In prayer-poems tinged with wonder, joy, humanness, and questioning, the author speaks for all of us who are groping and learning together what it means to be God's child. 07-3819-5

MORE THAN A CARPENTER by Josh McDowell. A hard-hitting book for people who are skeptical about Jesus' deity, his resurrection, and his claim on their lives. 07-4552-3

MOUNTAINS OF SPICES by Hannah Hurnard. Here is an allegory comparing the nine spices mentioned in the Song of Solomon to the nine fruits of the Spirit. A story of the glory of surrender by the author of **Hinds' Feet on High Places**. 07-4611-2

OUT OF THE STORM by Grace Livingston Hill. Gail finds herself afloat on an angry sea, desperately trying to keep an unconscious man from slipping away from her. 07-4778-X

QUICK TO LISTEN, SLOW TO SPEAK by Robert E. Fisher. Families are shown how to express love to one another by developing better listening skills, finding ways to disagree without arguing, and using constructive criticism. 07-5111-6

THE SECRET OF LOVING by Josh McDowell. McDowell explores the values and qualities that will help both single and married readers to be the right person for someone else. He offers a fresh perspective for evaluating and improving the reader's love life. 07-5845-5

Other Living Books Best-Sellers

STRIKE THE ORIGINAL MATCH by Charles Swindoll. Many couples ask: What do you do when the warm, passionate fire that once lit your marriage begins to wane? Here, Chuck Swindoll provides biblical steps for rekindling the fires of romance and building marital intimacy. 07-6445-5

SUCCESS! THE GLENN BLAND METHOD by Glenn Bland. The author shows how to set goals and make plans that really work. His ingredients of success include spiritual, financial, educational, and recreational balances. 07-6689-X

WHAT WIVES WISH THEIR HUSBANDS KNEW ABOUT WOMEN by James Dobson. The best-selling author of **Dare to Discipline** and **The Strong-Willed Child** brings us this vital book that speaks to the unique emotional needs and aspirations of today's woman. An immensely practical, interesting guide. 07-7896-0

WINDOW TO MY HEART by Joy Hawkins. A collection of heartfelt poems aptly expressing common emotions and thoughts that single women of any age experience. The author's vital trust in a loving God is evident throughout. 07-7977-0

If you are unable to find any of these titles at your local bookstore, you may call Tyndale's toll-free number **1-800-323-9400, X-214** for ordering information. Or you may write for pricing to **Tyndale Family Products, P.O. Box 448, Wheaton, IL 60189-0448.**